The Cambridge Manuals of Science and
Literature

MILITARY HISTORY

T0364336

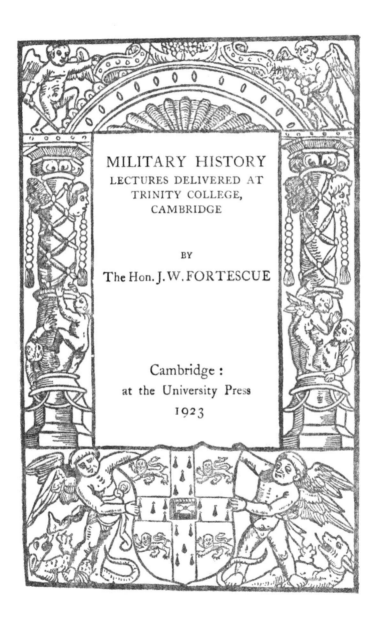

MILITARY HISTORY
LECTURES DELIVERED AT
TRINITY COLLEGE,
CAMBRIDGE

BY

The Hon. J. W. FORTESCUE

Cambridge :
at the University Press
1923

CAMBRIDGE UNIVERSITY PRESS
Cambridge, New York, Melbourne, Madrid, Cape Town,
Singapore, São Paulo, Delhi, Tokyo, Mexico City

Cambridge University Press
The Edinburgh Building, Cambridge CB2 8RU, UK

Published in the United States of America by Cambridge University Press, New York

www.cambridge.org
Information on this title: www.cambridge.org/9781107605848

© Cambridge University Press 1914

First Edition 1914
Reprinted 1923
First paperback edition 2011

A catalogue record for this publication is available from the British Library

ISBN 978-1-107-60584-8 Paperback

*With the exception of the coat of arms at
the foot, the design on the title page is a
reproduction of one used by the earliest
known Cambridge printer, John Siberch, 1521*

PREFACE

THERE is little in these lectures, or at any rate in three out of four of them, which I have not written at greater length in other volumes. I therefore publish them unwillingly, and in deference only to the wishes of some of my audience, whose good opinion I greatly value, and whose kindly sympathy I shall never forget. If this little volume should set but one student thinking seriously as to the meaning of military history, its object will be fully accomplished.

The spelling of Indian names has been, as usual, a stumbling-block. No doubt I shall be asked why I have used the form *Narbada* for the more familiar *Nerbuddha*, and yet written *Hyder Ali* instead of *Haidar Ali*. I can only say that when the form *Kalkáta* (or whatever may be the Hunterian spelling) is substituted for *Calcutta*, I shall be prepared to plead guilty to inconsistency.

J. W. F.

March 1914.

CONTENTS

LECTURE I

WHEN in the spring of the year 1913 my old College did me the honour to appoint me its first lecturer in Military History, I was obliged for the first time to ask myself seriously, What is military history? I confess that I have found it very difficult to furnish a satisfactory answer. Some would reply with a light heart that military history is the history of wars and warring. But what, in its turn, is war? It has been defined as an instrument of policy for the imposition of the will of one community upon another by force of arms. The definition is not a bad one. But *force of arms* is a very vague term, and must not be taken necessarily to imply an *armed force* in the ordinary acceptation of the words. You will remember that after the French fleet had been swept by us from the seas in 1805, Napoleon, unable to attack England by any other means, decreed the exclusion of British manufactures from the Continent, and endeavoured to ruin her by shutting her out of her markets. This he was able to do

because his previous conquests had placed the control
of many of the principal ports on the Continent in his
hands.   But though he strove thus to inflict his will
upon England by might of arms, the armed men necessary for enforcing it were nothing more formidable
than a small body of Custom-house officers. No doubt
these functionaries, or some of them, carried weapons
and in case of need were prepared to use them ;
but they cannot be considered as a military body.
None the less as an act of war the Continental System
was a bitter and deadly stroke, which nearly proved
successful.

Is the history of the Continental System, therefore, military history ?   So far as concerns the invasion of Spain, Portugal and Russia to coerce those
countries into the acceptance of it, undoubtedly it is.
But as regards England, the power at which it was
really aimed, what are we to say of it ?   How did we
endeavour to combat it ?   How does any country
invariably combat the commercial restrictions of any
other ?   First by imposing retaliatory restrictions
of her own, or engaging in a war of blockades or
tariffs, which may be called regular commercial
warfare ;   secondly, by the practice of smuggling,
which may be called irregular commercial warfare.
Is the history of a war of tariffs, then, military
history ?   If we answer in the affirmative there is
no escape from the logical conclusion that the never-

ceasing contest between smugglers and revenue-officers in all countries is military history. Moreover, since revenue-officers are only departmental police, it follows that the external struggle between the breakers and the upholders of the law at large—between criminals and the police—is also military history. But this is to say that the history of social communities generally is military history; and I cannot think this to have been in the mind of the generous founder of the lecturership which I have the honour to hold.

But can we then lay down the general proposition that the breach—the forcible breach—of commercial regulations is not military history? I do not think we can, if we bear in mind how Spain, in virtue of a Papal bull, excluded all other nations from commerce with the new world, and how successive Englishmen for many generations insisted upon flouting her. Nor can we say that in many cases the conflict between supporters and breakers of the law is not military history. It is merely a question of degree. A fight between three drunken men and the police is a scuffle. A fight between three hundred men and the police is a riot. A fight between three hundred thousand and the police is civil war; and we cannot exclude civil war from military history, for it would mean the sacrifice, among the English-speaking race alone, of the campaigns of Cromwell,

George Washington and Robert Lee. Altogether I
think that we must abandon the attempt to define
military history as the history of wars and warring.
I feel tempted to ask in despair not " What is military
history ? " but rather " What is *not* military history?"
since all history is but the record of the strife of men
for the subsistence of their bodies or the prevalence
of their opinions.   But we must be patient for yet a
little while, and try once more.

Let us begin, then, by laying it down provisionally
that military history is the history of the strife of
communities. This is not enough ; for communities
have been known before now to fight with anathemas,
and such a conflict belongs rather to the domain of
religious than of military history. Shall we say then
that it is the history of the strife of communities for
self-preservation or expansion ? This is open to the
obvious criticism that communities have fought and
will fight again for many other objects than the two
above-mentioned—for a woman, for a creed, for a
principle moral or political, or even for nothing at all
but from sheer force of habit. So it will be wiser
for us to avoid any specification of the objects of
strife, or we may find ourselves in trouble. It may
be true in a sense to say that a tantrum of Madame
de Pompadour cost the French their empire in North
America and in India ; but it is not the whole truth,
nor nearly the whole truth. Even the best and

greatest of historians are but gropers in a thick darkness, and epigrams are the most deceitful of will-o'-the-wisps.

Let us now, as we needs must, strengthen our definition a little, and say that military history is the history of the strife of communities expressed through the conflict of organised bands of armed men. I am obliged to say *bands* of armed men so as to exclude such a case as a duel between two or more chosen champions of quarrelling communities; and I add the word *organised* so as to indicate that, below a certain stage of civilisation, there can be no military history. This is a second definition, but still imperfect; and I am afraid that I cannot yet improve it. It leaves a vast field for the survey of a lecturer, far vaster than I have the knowledge to cover; and, if Trinity should endure for another ten centuries, my successors will never want material for interesting and instructive lectures. And let no man persuade you that the subject is trivial or unimportant—that the study of war is the study of a relic of barbarism to be eschewed by the serious, the devout and the humane. I am not denying that war is a terrible—from some points of view even a hideous—thing. Since its object is to compel a number of people to do what they do not wish, by making their lives a burden to them, it must sometimes be a hideous thing. But, after all, the system

of forcing people to observe a certain line of conduct under penalties is that upon which all human
society is founded. We are all subject to it at this
moment, and have been from the beginning of our
lives. You remember the mother in *Punch*—
" Go and see what baby is doing, and tell her she
mustn't." " Thou shalt not " is the basis of four-
fifths of the ancient code of law which is most
familiar to us, and of all other codes since. But
in every community there are a certain number of
individuals who answer " Thou shalt not " with
a resolute " I will " ; and these we ostracise, or
imprison, or hang. We call such people lunatics
or criminals, accordingly as we consider them
responsible or not responsible for their actions,
and we treat them as we think that they deserve ;
but, if by chance their opinions should later prevail even for a time, we proclaim them apostles or
martyrs. There is, in fact, always the danger
that, when we think ourselves to be merely punish-
ing a criminal, we may really be torturing a great
reformer. Hence a certain proportion of folks
among us shrink from this system of coercion,
and would have no government at all. Others
again, looking upon the existence of private property as the main reason for the existence of the
policeman, would have communities share all things
in common. I mention these facts to show you

that the employment of force receives from some thinkers equal condemnation, whether to impose the will of a community upon its own citizens, or upon those of some other community.

But no one on that account has ventured to stigmatize the study of penal codes, and of the organisation for putting them into force, as ignoble or unprofitable. The sheriff, for instance, and his functions are approached with respect, by some historians even with awe. "Ah," say the despisers of military history, "but the sheriff is an instrument for compelling obedience to the law, not the leader of a host whose business it is to slaughter and destroy." The law! and what is the law but the formulated will which some section of the community, possibly a majority, but always in former days and frequently, even at present, a minority, seeks to impose upon the whole? And if breakers of the law resist the sheriff or policeman, will he not if necessary slaughter them, and destroy any shelter in which they may have taken refuge? Of course he will, and "the law" will uphold him for so doing. "But," reply the objectors, "you forget that civil law is not always a mere ordinance of man; it may have the sanction of divine authority." I speak here with all reverence, but how many are the armies and the leaders that have claimed that theirs was the cause of God,

and have fared forth to war in His name ? I am not
speaking now of modern armies, though they too
invariably invoke the help of the God of Battles,
and call him to witness that their cause is just.
Look at the Crusades on one side, look on the
other at the mighty and overwhelming conquests
of Islam. Look at the extinction of Christianity in
North Africa ; look at the eight centuries of conflict
which banished the Mohammedan faith from Spain.
Look at the religious wars of Christians in Europe ;
and not least at our own Puritans. Look finally
at the bitter struggles of Hindu and Mohammedan
in India. There was not one of these parties that
did not claim, that did not for the most part heartily
believe, that it was fighting to uphold the law of
God.

No ! in its essence there is no difference between
the force that imposes the will of a man upon his
neighbour, and that which imposes his will upon
his enemy. In the more primitive days of England
the duties of the sheriff and his *posse comitatus* extended to foreign enemies on English soil as well as
to domestic law-breakers. Do we not to this day
speak of those guilty of acts of violence as *breakers
of the King's Peace* ; men, that is, who seek to bring
about a state of war and must be suppressed by the
methods of war—taken prisoners, wounded or un-
wounded, and in the last resort killed ? What was

the origin of our own standing army ? It was
formed, as you doubtless know, out of a remnant
of the victorious army of the Parliament which had
overthrown the monarchy, a remnant which was
saved from disbandment in order to overawe the
turbulent of London, or in other words to serve as
a body of police. It continued to be the only
efficient instrument for imposing the will of the
Government upon the people until 1829, when the
present police-force was established. And the
police are a standing army, neither more or less.
The only essential difference between police and
soldiers is that the former are employed mainly in
the coercion of subjects of the State which levies
them, while the function of the latter is to coerce
the subjects of foreign states. It would not be
inaccurate to say that police are soldiers against
domestic enemies, and an army police against
foreign enemies.

And now observe that we have found a second
definition of military history. It is the history of
the external police of communities and nations.
But external police, you may object, implies the
existence of something which, for want of a better
word, we must call external law. Is there such a
thing as external law ? There is a thing called the
law of nations or international law, which is concerned chiefly, though not exclusively, with the

relations between belligerents and neutrals, but which is simply custom, and should not be called law, because there is no international police to enforce it. Any nation may defy it, if she thinks it worth while, and a great many have defied it in the past and will defy it in the future, not necessarily with any damage to themselves. The same may be said of the International Tribunal of Arbitration at the Hague. Its decrees and decisions may be excellent, and nations may bind themselves beforehand to accept them ; but nations are not remarkable for the observance of inconvenient agreements, where there is no penalty for violating them. It is a painful fact, but in its relations to its neighbours every community is a law unto itself, the nature of that law being principally determined by the community's powers of enforcement. Police first, law afterwards, is the rule between nation and nation—a formula which may be rendered more tersely still by the phrase, Might is Right. In a sense, therefore, though not in the sense generally attached to the words, military history is the history of the law of nations, which is the law of force ; or, if you prefer it, of the law of force which is the law of nations.

A revolting thought, perhaps some of you will say ! Have all the efforts of countless generations of good and holy men to seek peace and ensue it, resulted in no greater success than this ? Let us

have the courage to face facts and answer boldly,
Yes ; for be very sure that no piety of aspiration
can dignify nor excuse the moral cowardice that
seeks to evade them. You know that late in the
17th century a company of worthy and excellent
men formed the settlement of Pennsylvania in
North America. They were members of the Society
of Friends, who would have nothing to do with
war, and consequently bought their lands from the
Indians instead of taking them by force or fraud.
Frugal, thrifty and industrious, they soon grew
wealthy, and extended their borders further and
further, until they came into collision with other
tribes of Indians, who one day fell upon the out-
lying settlers with fire and sword. In utter dismay
the sufferers appealed to the Government of the
province for protection ; but the Colonial Assembly
would not do violence to their tenets and ignored
the appeal, leaving their unhappy and inoffensive
frontiersmen to be massacred. At length, goaded
to desperation, the settlers came down to Philadelphia with their arms in their hands, and
threatened violence unless the Assembly voted
money, for supply of ammunition, and other measures
of defence forthwith. Thereupon the Assembly
yielded, but still they would not openly pass a vote
for the purchase of gunpowder. To save their
conscience they voted money only for the purchase

of corn or *other grain*, which, as gunpowder is made
up of grains, was sufficient warrant for the acquisi-
tion of the necessary but unspeakable article.   To
such contemptible subterfuge are men driven who
refuse to face facts.   I understand the feelings of
those who deplore that the government of human
society should rest ultimately upon force, but I
have no patience with those who pretend that it
does not.   It can profit no man to be obliged so to
shape the actions of his life that they may square
with a fundamental lie.

Accepting then the fact—for such I believe it to
be—that the law of nations is the law of force, let
us waste no time in lamentations.   In the first
place they are useless ; and in the second they seem
to me highly presumptuous ; for what are we, or
what is our knowledge, that we should aspire to
correct the course of this world's governance ?
Let us rather consider what is meant by the word
force, as an element in the conflict of communities.
Force, in the human creature, is of two kinds,
moral and physical ; and in war, as Napoleon himself said, the moral is to the physical as four to one.
What is this moral force ?   It is an indefinable con-
sciousness of superiority.   And whence does it arise ?
I must summon a poet to help me with my answer.

> "Self-reverence, self-knowledge, self-control,
> These three alone lead life to sovereign power."

Self-reverence, which can be based only upon high
aspirations and high ideals ; self-knowledge, which
combines the courage to face facts, the patience to
accept them, the constancy to turn them to good
account ; self-control, the offspring of self-denial
and self-discipline. We are too much inclined to
think of war as a matter of combats, demanding
above all things physical courage. It is really a
matter of fasting and thirsting ; of toiling and
waking ; of lacking and enduring ; which demands
above all things moral courage. Yet let us hasten
to add that, without bodily soundness and strength
to resist privation, hardship and fatigue, an army
is naught. And here we strike the peculiarity
which makes war the true touch-stone of nations.
It is the supreme test of their merits and demerits
both moral and physical. By a community's art,
literature, science and philosophy you may take the
measure of its intellectual attainments ; through
its administrative institutions and laws you may
form some judgment of its political intelligence ;
from the bodily structure and condition of its
citizens you may form conclusions as to its physical
fitness ; but of the general soundness of the body
politic, of the capacity of its leaders, of the devotion
of their followers, of the moral force which inspires
all ages and both sexes to endure hardship and
sorrow with cheerfulness, and to meet adversity

with confidence unshaken and with courage undaunted—for all this the trial of all trials is war.

Military history is the history of these trials.
Does it seem to you a small, or ignoble, or unprofitable thing ?   But, it may be objected, this is an
unfair way of putting the matter.   No doubt it
may be profitable to compare the political institutions of some effete community with those of the
young, virile and vigorous communities which swept
it out of existence.   But the details of fire and sword,
of massacre and devastation, of the blood of men
and the tears of women, are they profitable ?   And
the elaborate principles of strategy and tactics—
that is to say the bringing of the armed force up to
the field of decision, and the handling of it to the
best advantage when there ;   with their ancillary
sciences of fortification and poliorketics, that is to
say, of setting up strong places and knocking them
down again—are they profitable ?   What are the
art of war and the science of military organisation
but the art and science of destruction ?   Can the
study of these be profitable ?

Let us clear our minds of cant.   What is the
economy of this world, so far as we have eyes to see
and intellects to understand it, but destruction and
renewal, destruction and renewal ?   And it is really
impossible, except by our petty human standards,
to distinguish the one from the other.   I have seen

—and perhaps some of you may have seen the like—
what we call a desert, of a thousand square miles of
pumice-stone. This pumice-stone is a layer which
varies from six to fifteen feet in depth ; and below
it lie the trunks of gigantic trees, all black and
charred, which were scathed and overthrown by the
same terrific volcanic explosion which afterwards
buried them in pumice. The soil must have been
fertile to raise such trees ; and men lament the
destruction which has made so large an area into
a waste. But what they mean by *destruction* and
waste is simply the change which has rendered it
useless, so far as they can see, for purposes of
producing food and exchangeable commodities immediately to the profit of *men*—that and nothing
more. Whether it be destruction or renewal in
the scheme of nature we cannot tell. But let us
pass to the works of man, the great destroyer.
What does a field of corn mean but that the plants
which originally grew there have been ruthlessly
destroyed to make way for those that better suit
the purposes of man, and that an unknown quantity
of animal life, dependent upon the plants so destroyed, has perished with them ? What does a
herd of cattle in a field mean but the destruction
of all wild cattle, till these became tame enough to
await their turn of destruction for the service of
man ? And as with plants and the inferior animals,

so does man deal with man. He endeavours to destroy those that do not suit his purpose, and to replace them by others. And this he does by many other methods besides those which we group under the name of war. Within the memory of living men there were many excellent but simple gentlemen who thought that what is called Free Trade would soon be adopted by every civilised country in the world, and that then wars would cease. The prediction has not been verified, nor can I see that the world would be very much the better if it had been. For commerce is not, as is generally supposed, a peaceful pursuit. What does successful commerce mean? The under-selling of competitors; which means in turn cheaper production than is possible to competitors. But cheap production, other things being equal, depends in these days chiefly upon two things—cheap labour, which means low wages, and the best of machinery. Who can tell how many lives have been sacrificed to low wages in the winning of any commercial competition; or how many men, women and children have been starved when machinery, either absolutely or practically new, has driven a mass of bread-winners out of employment? And these are the casualties only on the victorious side. What have they been on the beaten side, when whole industries have been ruined? If we could arrive at a just estimate of the

casualty lists filled by commerce, I doubt greatly
if they would be lower than those filled by war.
Improved machinery, in the case of a great many
manufactures, is as truly an engine of destruction
as a torpedo or a heavy gun. It is meant to destroy
other competing machinery and to drive its work-
men from it, just as a torpedo is meant to destroy
a ship and send its crew to the bottom. A town
deserted and falling to ruin owing to loss of trade
and consequent loss of population, is as truly destroyed as if it had been battered to pieces by shot
and shell.

This, it may be said, is an unkind way of stating
the matter. The superior machinery supplants
and replaces the inferior. Quite so. There is in
a general way renewal as well as destruction ; but
the superior machinery does not replace the men
who have perished in assuring its triumph on the
one side, or in succumbing to that triumph on the
other. And after all what is the general purport
of war but to replace what is inferior by what is
superior ? What are the rise and fall of civilisa-
tions, empires, states, nations and communities,
but the process of supplanting the inferior by the
superior, or at any rate the subjection of the inferior
to the superior ? Military history is the history of that
process, and it is no more the history of destruction
than any other kind of history. I do not suppose

that the most tender-hearted member of the Society
of Friends would take exception to the study of
the legislative enactments whereby, quite apart
from warlike measures, we wrested their former
commercial superiority from the Dutch. He would
not call it a history of destruction, and yet it was
so—to the Dutch. In the case of a military war
the casualty lists are published, and everyone says
"How shocking." In the case of a commercial
war it is announced that such and such a firm has
closed its works through bankruptcy; and few,
unless they chance to be share-holders, think more
about the matter. There may be some hundreds
of people deprived of their livelihood, but few
consider that. Military victors feed their prisoners
of war: commercial victors leave them to starve.
And yet commerce is held to be humane, and war
very much the contrary; while captains of industry
are held in honour by men to whom the fame of a
captain in war gives sincere and conscientious
affliction.

Thus you see how futile, however well-intended,
are peace-societies and similar institutions, inasmuch
as they recognise only one description—the military—of war. It is terrible to think how true is
the saying of Erasmus, *Homo homini lupus*. We
like to be successful ourselves, and we like our
friends to be successful also, but we seldom reflect

that every success is won at the cost of another's failure. Even here in Cambridge, and among those merriest of mortals, undergraduates, the stern inexorable law asserts itself. For one whom a class-list makes happy, how many does it make miserable ? For one to whom it offers the prospect of food and warmth, to how many does it threaten cold and want ? *Homo homini lupus*, that is individual history. *Gentes gentibus lupi*, that is universal history.

But to return to a question which I have still left unanswered, wherein lies the profit for men not of the military profession, of studying the principles and the history of war, with the terrible details in which the history abounds so frequently ? One chief profit, as I take it, is to learn the nature of the supreme test to which a nation may be subjected, so that she may equip herself morally and physically to pass through the ordeal with success. Let me repeat to you that war is less a matter of courage than of endurance. Of really brave men, men who from sheer love of fighting cannot be kept out of fire, the proportion is about one in a thousand. Of real cowards, men who literally cannot be induced to face fire in any circumstances, the proportion is about the same. The remainder can by training and discipline be brought to do their duty with more or less bravery, which is sufficient—or at any rate must be considered sufficient—for the purpose. Such training and discipline are a purely military matter, to which I shall presently return. But endurance depends upon moral and physical attributes which, though a great leader or regimental pride may do much to enhance them, are principally the concern of the statesman. Let us deal first with the physical requirements of a soldier.

First and foremost he must be mature, a man and not a boy ; otherwise, no matter how great his pluck, he will never be able to withstand the hard work of a campaign. There is hardly a country which has not again and again filled up its muster-rolls with children, and deceived itself into the belief that it was enlarging its armies, instead of filling up its military hospitals and graveyards. Boys can of course do the work of garrisons within certain limits ; but it is (to speak brutally) cheaper to knock them on the head at once and bury them at home than to send them upon active service in the field. On the other hand, men must not be too old, otherwise they succumb to rheumatic complaints in consequence of exposure to cold and wet. For the rest, the soundness of the feet, in order that men may be able to march ; of the eyes, so that they may be able to see ; and of the teeth, are of the greatest importance. An enormous proportion of men on active service die of dysentery or enteric fever, due to bad and ill-cooked food ; and want of teeth to masticate that food aggravates the evil immensely. Bad sight and bad teeth are very common in the inhabitants of large towns, as also of course is inferior physique generally. Such defects weaken a nation for war ; and a wise government will not let them continue without endeavouring to arrest them.

But, apart from this, much may often be done by care and foresight to abate the hardships of a campaign. It is often inevitable that the men's clothing should be in rags, and their feet almost if not quite shoeless for a time ; as also that they should be scantily fed and then not on the best of food ; but, if this be borne in mind, and measures taken to keep abundant supplies of everything at the seat of war, together with transport to convey such supplies to the front, privation and suffering may be greatly lessened, and sickness proportionately decreased. People who have never studied military history do not realise that a campaign is a gigantic picnic, and that, unless careful arrangement be made long beforehand for every detail of food, forage, clothing and carriage, an army may perish before it can reach its enemy. Such arrangement involves a nicety of organisation of which the ordinary civilian never dreams. One great lesson therefore that all may learn from

the study of military history is, that the casualties
through lead and steel are a trifle to those from
hardship and the resultant sickness; and that
these last may be very appreciably diminished by
experience, forethought and organisation.

So much for the purely physical side of an army.
The question of inspiring it with moral force could
easily lead me into an endless disquisition upon the
merits of different forms of civil government and
different systems of education. I shall not be so
foolish as to attempt anything of the kind; but I
shall content myself with stating that the great
secret of an army's moral force is that (in Cromwell's
words) all ranks shall " know what they are fighting
for, and love what they know." The most powerful of all purely moral forces is undoubtedly religious
fanaticism, of which many instances will at once occur
to you; but I question if among all its countless
manifestations there are any quite so thorough as are
found in the hosts of Islam. There are many
instances of desperate courage and devotion among
all races and all creeds, but I do not know where
you will find a parallel, except in the annals of
Mohammedan warfare, to the attack of the hordes
of the Khalifa at Omdurman.

Another great moral force is political fanaticism;
but as a rule there underlies all combative fanaticism,
either consciously or unconsciously, that less exalted

element of human nature which is known as greed.
Greed of course is of many kinds. It may arise from
honest hunger and poverty ; or from the less honourable, though hardly less cogent, persuasion that
those who have are the legitimate prey of those
who have not. But its manifestations are uniformly the same, though they are often embellished
by titles of honour. People who would not dream
of robbing their neighbours, if the process were
described to them in as many words, will take
credit to themselves for spoiling the heathen or the
Amalekites. Primitive tribes and clans, which have
outgrown or exhausted the territory that at one
time sufficed for their support, are not always so
squeamish. They see a weak and prosperous neighbour, fall upon him without more ado, and eat
him up. Christian nations and Mohammedans have
frequently extinguished aboriginal tribes as heretics
and unbelievers. We ourselves used to excuse our
predatory excursions against the Spaniards upon
the ground that Popish idolators deserved nothing
better. Turn now to a case which is generally ad-
duced as an example of an army inspired by political
fanaticism—the levies which burst out from France
against her neighbours on all sides in 1792 and 1793.
They came, as they proclaimed, to carry the gospel
of liberty, equality and fraternity into all lands ;
their evangel was to be for the healing of the nations ;

they menaced war only to the nobleman's castle ;
they brought peace to the poor man's cottage.
Were they really inspired by any such exalted senti-
ments ? A few enthusiasts may have been; but
not many. Did their faith in their new creed
suffice to make them die for it cheerfully ? Not
in the least ; for they ran away like sheep, until
habit and discipline inured them to war. Did they
conduct themselves, where successful, according to
their noble professions ? Not in the least. They
plundered all classes impartially, and were loathed
by all impartially. The truth is that their real
object was not to preach a gospel at all, but to
gather plunder. France had been ruined by the
incredible follies of the Revolution ; her resources
were exhausted ; and there was nothing for her
but to rob her neighbours or perish. Her robberies
prospered ; a soldier of fortune rose up to take
command of her armies ; and under his leadership
the principle of robbery was indefinitely extended.
As Wellington put it with his usual shrewd insight,
war to Napoleon was a financial resource.

Must hope of plunder then be reckoned as a
great moral force in war ? The question is extremely difficult to answer. Astonishing military
successes have been achieved under no other stimu-
lating influence than this—I would instance the
sack of Rome by Charles of Bourbon in 1527—but

plunder, speaking generally, demoralises both the army and the nation that lives by it, for it leads to jealousy and divisions. You will remember at once, when I recall it to you, the story in the Old Testament of Saul's preservation of flocks, herds and prisoners in the face of Samuel's order that they should be annihilated. I strongly suspect that Samuel's motive for commanding the destruction of the plunder was apprehension lest the King, by offering to his followers a reward for their services, should steal away the hearts of the people and undermine the authority of the priesthood. On the other hand Saul may perhaps have been justified in supposing that his men would not fight the Amalekites without the assurance of a share in the spoil, and had consequently promised them a share beforehand. At any rate, it is certain that the incident so far estranged the ecclesiastical from the civil authorities that the former put forward a rival to oust Saul from the Kingship. This is a curious instance of an entire community being driven into civil war by a dispute as to plunder. Of its demoralising influence on an army the examples are endless, but I may mention to you the furious combats of the Spaniards and Germans over the spoil of Rome, which they had combined to capture and sack ; the practical dissolution for a time of Wellington's troops after the storm of Badajoz, and the insubordination and disunion of Napoleon's armies in Spain, when nearly every officer of rank was seeking to enrich himself, and employing his men to enrich him, instead of using them in the legitimate operations of war.

Nevertheless men will not go a-fighting continuously unless there is plunder, or some composition in lieu thereof, to stimulate them to constant exertion. In the fifteenth and sixteenth centuries the military profession was very nearly a mercantile affair, pure and simple. Capitalists formed companies of soldiers for hire, and sought to indemnify themselves by plunder for their venture, very much after the fashion of a privateer or private man-of-war. The " purchase-system " under which, when I was a boy, British officers still purchased their commissions for a sum of money, was a relic of the old practice of buying shares in a military company. In many of our wars there was no individual plunder, but all captures were lumped together, sold, and divided in due proportion between all ranks of the army engaged. The army which stormed Seringapatam in 1799 divided £1,300,000 in this way ; and beyond all doubt the hope of large profits was a great incentive to the men to endure many things and fight hard. Soldiers are almost invariably ill-paid. Very often their health is permanently impaired by the hardship and privation which they undergo ; and they demand, not unreasonably, some compensation for all their sufferings and peril. This is a fact which no statesman can afford to overlook. Even in the middle of the late South African war it was necessary to give to every private five pounds, and to every non-commissioned officer and officer still larger sums, according to their rank, as prize money in lieu of plunder.

I come next to patriotism as a moral force. We are apt to take it for granted that it always exists in every country ; but this is not so, as the earlier wars of the French Revolution most plainly prove. Nor is it sufficient to say that the countries over which the French armies rode rough-shod were autocratically governed, while France enjoyed a freer form of government, for a democracy can, and very frequently does, govern quite as abominably as any autocrat or oligarchy. If a large proportion of a community be discontented with its condition it will feel no patriotism, and will do little or nothing towards defence of its country. It sees no object in fighting to maintain a state of things which it disapproves, and will not do so. Then, in case of invasion it will submit quietly and without an effort to the enemy's will, and allow him to take peaceful possession of its territory. If, on the contrary, the war be not defensive but offensive, the malcontents will lay themselves out to embarrass the ruling

authorities as much as possible, in order to secure
political changes which they conceive to be political
advantages. So long as the seat of operations is at
a distance, the behaviour of the malcontents is
always the same, whether they are of the highest
or of the lowest class, whether the government
under which they live be popular or despotic.
Thus during the American War of Independence a
considerable section of the English aristocracy
threw the whole weight of its power and influence
in favour of the revolting colonies, and to all intents
assured their triumph. Thus also in the recent
war between Russia and Japan a large section of
the educated classes in Russia spared no efforts to
stir up internal trouble, and crippled their country
at the very moment when she bade fair to redeem
all past failures and enter upon a successful campaign. In both cases the disaffected parties claimed
to be the truest patriots, inasmuch as they had
acted in the best interests of their country; though
whether such a claim can be justified is a matter
upon which men will differ until the end of time.
It may, however, be doubted whether men can,
unless in most exceptional circumstances, benefit
their country by seconding their country's enemies;
and it is probable that, when they profess to do so,
they are animated rather by an intense desire to
injure and humiliate their rulers than by any

principle of well-doing towards any one. If the war were brought home to their own hearths, they would in all likelihood make a stubborn fight for their defence ; either from dread lest their neighbours should hang them ; or, as it is more reasonable to suppose, from honest jealousy for their country and indignation against the invader. But because the scene of fighting is at a distance, they think that they may legitimately play fast and loose with their country's fortunes.

Now I cannot help thinking that if those who aspire to govern men, and even to lay claim to the title of statesmen, were to study military history, they might learn enough about the moral force of nations and armies to set them thinking very seriously. It is a force that is very difficult to build up and not very difficult to destroy ; and yet politicians of all parties trifle with it as though it were an insignificant matter. It is impossible to devise a form of Government or to collect an administration which will satisfy all men ; but, though everyone recognises the fact in theory, few make allowances for it in practice. It is sufficient for politicians of all ways of thinking in these days to say solemnly that the will of the majority must prevail. But why must it prevail ? Because the majority is more likely to be right than the minority ? Far from it : if we could believe that this were the

rule, the government of the world would be much
easier than it is.   No, the will of the majority must
prevail because it can be enforced on the minority,
which is only another way of saying that Might is
Right.   See how in this world of cant the terrible
maxim, which men think applicable to war only, is
daily in force all round us.   Wise men therefore will
be always moderate in their dealing with honest
and respectable minorities, whether they differ
from the majority in matters of religious, political
or social faith, provided always that their dissent
is not merely a cloak for evading the obligations
of ordinary morality.   Yet such moderation, though
of the last importance towards amity and good understanding in a community and therefore towards its
moral force in the event of war, is little more common
to-day than at other periods of human history.   There
is really only one political or social principle which
has any permanent worth, and it is expressed in
the homely proverb " Give and take."

What is the civic form of this proverb ?   It is
this, No rights without duties, no duties without
rights.   In England I am afraid—though I may be
wrong—that for some time past there has been too
much prating of rights, and too little reflection upon
duties; though the commonwealth depends for its
stability upon the equal recognition of both.   What,
you may ask, do you owe to the State ?   Well, you

owe to it gratitude for the fact that you can for the most part walk about decently clad and purse in pocket without danger of being knocked on the head ; and that you can pursue your lawful avocation in peace. But how if your clothes are in rags and you have no purse ? Well then, apart from all possible benefits from the poor law, you at least enjoy immunity from being knocked on the head as an unprofitable member of the tribe. The great difference between primitive and civilised societies is that the civilised recognise misfortune as a palliative to inefficiency, which the primitive cannot afford to do. We have still a right to say that a criminal is an inefficient citizen, but no longer that an inefficient citizen is a criminal ; and this, for some of us, is a considerable gain. Even if the State gave us no more than this, we are everyone of us debtors for more than we can repay. But, in the most highly organised states of the present time, the tendency is that the community at large shall contribute more and more towards making men physically and mentally into efficient citizens and towards saving them from the consequences of misfortune, but in return shall claim from them more exacting duties. It would perhaps be historically more accurate to say that in some cases the duties came first and the benefits afterwards ; but the point is that the principle of rights for duties and

duties for rights has been faithfully observed.
Thus in Germany the State has set up machinery
for education, for insurance against misfortune,
for provision against old age, claiming in return
from able-bodied citizens two years of military
training, with liability to be recalled to the colours
up to a certain age in the event of war. There
are other states in which the same or less is given
or claimed ; but there are few of importance in
Europe in which free education is not the right,
and military training the countervailing duty.
And this system has been adopted in every case,
not only from bitter experience of disastrous defeat
in war, but because foreign statesmen read military
history. The bond of a common duty, impartially
imposed upon all classes from the highest to the
lowest, tends to soften minor differences and dis-
contents, and constitutes in itself a great moral
force.

So much for the moral force that can be instilled
into a community by its statesmen : I come now to
that which can be inspired only by the soldier, the
unity, artificial but incomparably strong, which is
bound up with the name of discipline. Military
discipline—how some people loathe and others
worship it ; and how little the majority of both
have really thought about it ! What is its principle ?
The organised abnegation of the individual self in

favour of the corporate self. What is its object ?
That tens of thousands may act together as one
under the guidance of a single will. What are its
methods ?   Immediate and unquestioning obedience to superior command.   Immediate and
unquestioning obedience—that is what is the
stumbling block, the *skandalon* to so many. There
are of course a certain number of people who can
obey no one, but must always be a law—and an
exceedingly erratic law—unto themselves. The
name of the poet Shelley will probably occur to
some of you, but I am not thinking of such as
Shelley. I have in my mind rather those excellent
but generally unthinking persons who shrink with
horror from the idea of a man's abdicating his civil
rights. "What," they say, "a man must obey
even an unjust command, under pain it may be of
death ! It is monstrous ! " For purposes of civil
life it might be monstrous, but not for purposes of
implicit obedience, which is the thing that matters
in an army. Let there be justice as far as possible
by all means ; but, as a general principle, it is better
for an army that an injustice should be done than
that an order should be disobeyed. This, however,
is an argument that cannot appeal to our imaginary
objector, because he has read no military history.

Then there is the unpleasant fact that immediate and unquestioning obedience is a thing not

easily acquired even with the best of good will. Careful and often tedious training is necessary before the obedience becomes instinctive and a second nature ; and the process is not always a pleasant one. In the first place tyrannical teachers are always to be found, who make the lesson as odious as possible ; and in the second there are some natures to which nothing is so revolting as order and method in the minutest detail. The temperament that calls itself artistic is particularly impatient of this description of discipline, and attaches to it the name of soul-destroying ; but I have noticed that persons who claim to possess that particular temperament discover equal mischief to their souls in the punctual keeping of their appointments, the faithful fulfilment of their contracts, and the regular payment of their debts. In fact a little drill and discipline is the very thing that they most require. However, the school of implicit obedience is no doubt a hard one, and sometimes even distressing. There is much that seems—perhaps even a little that may actually be—unnecessary and pedantic in the instruction ; and in time of peace the necessity for this is not obvious. It is inexpressibly galling to some characters to find the question *Why* answered unchangeably by the formula " Because orders must be obeyed." They chafe against the compression of

all natures into the same mould; and the con-
version of one, who flatters himself (not always
with reason) that he is an intelligent mortal, into
a machine.

I shall deal with the weak side of military
discipline presently. Meanwhile observe that its
moral force is founded on one of the noblest of
human, I might say of Christian, virtues. I have
styled it organised self-abnegation—organised self-
surrender of the individual for the sake of the
general;—only possible through arduous training
in self-denial, self-restraint and self-control.
Observe that, although many religious orders have
taken for their governance the vows of poverty,
chastity and obedience, the most formidable of all
was that founded by an old soldier, who organised
it upon a military model and gave its chief the title
of General. The name of the Jesuits does not
smell sweet in English nostrils, and yet its members
have perhaps outdone all the world in self-sacrifice.
"Go," the General said from time to time to some
young Jesuit in the 17th century, "Go out to the
wilds of North America; spread the gospel among
the Red Indians; search out the land and take it
into possession for the most Christian king."
Without a word the command was obeyed. The
missionary went forth, alone or with a comrade,
undaunted by the prospect of being tied up to

roast before a slow fire, or have his fingers bitten
off one by one ; he dwelt among savage men, lived
their lives, subsisted on their food, and, without
counting the risk of being lost or starved, found
his way down the great rivers from the Upper Lakes
to the Gulf of Florida. You know the great examples of heroism in our own army. You know
the story of the *Birkenhead* ; and you may perhaps
realise that it is this story which has inspired all
English men and English women to show courage
in a shipwreck. But I shall add just one story, a
very short one, of the wreck of the *Warren Hastings*,
which was carrying four companies of the King's
Royal Rifle Corps and as many of the York and
Lancaster Regiment, on the island of Reunion in
1897. When the ship struck, sentries of the Rifles
were at once posted at various points on the lower
deck, to guard the access to the spirit-room and
such like ; and there they remained while the boats
were lowered to take the battalion ashore. The
water rose steadily upon them inch by inch, and
had reached their chests, when at last an officer
came to summon them also, last of all, to take their
place in the boats. He collected them all, as he
thought, but in the noise and darkness he missed
one man and left him behind. The man saw his
comrades disappear up the ladder, and the officer
about to follow them, and not till then did he ask,

without quitting his post, " Beg pardon, sir, may I
come too ? " If ever you hear any man speak
lightly of military discipline, tell him that story,
for that Rifleman is worthy to be placed alongside
the Roman sentry at Pompeii.

Yet it is very necessary that the working of
military discipline should be most carefully studied
in military history, in order that its defects, weak-
nesses and limitations may be thoroughly ascertained
and realised. There is no greater mistake than to
say that disciplined men are machines. They are
nothing of the kind : they are flesh and blood ;
and it is most dangerous to treat them as anything
else. Yet nothing is more common than for people
to suppose that anything is good enough for soldiers
because discipline forbids them to complain. Politicians in particular often appear to think that a
soldier, in virtue of his discipline, can march all
day and all night, dispense with food and drink,
and lie out in cold and rain with no particular
mischief to himself. I can assure you that in former
days, within the memory of living men, English
soldiers were housed in buildings and sent to sea
in vessels that would have been thought too bad
for valuable cattle. Tradesmen and contractors likewise presume upon the soldiers' enforced patience,
and mobs will insult and pelt them, secure in
the knowledge that the soldiers will not retaliate

without orders.   This indeed, albeit infinitely mean
and cowardly, is an unconscious tribute to discipline,
but may easily strain it beyond endurance.   The fact
is that discipline which rests wholly upon fear is
not the strongest.   Inelastic and unsympathetic
severity, even though it may not actually amount
to injustice, can produce only a passive and discontented obedience, which speedily gives way to
sulky insubordination under any unusual trial.
It is when officers are not in touch with their men
and do not consider them, that the hearts of soldiers
are stolen away by agitators and malcontents.   And
then follows mutiny, which if begun in some choice
corps may spread to a whole army, as in the French
Revolution, and bring a dynasty and the traditions
of centuries to the ground.   The ill-treatment of
men was common enough in old days, when the
gaps between social classes were wide and the distinction between them carefully marked, but you
will never find an instance of a successful army in
which the officers did not share the hardships of
the men.   Hannibal, for one, frequently slept on
the ground with his outposts.

It is when, as in most modern armies, the officers
put their men before anything else in the world,
that military discipline shines at its brightest.   This
does not mean leniency to irregularity or towards
insubordination—a weak or indulgent officer is

neither loved nor respected—but the treatment of
men as men instead of as children, attention to
their wants, consideration for their feelings, zeal
for their well-being, cultivation of their self-respect,
forethought to train them to meet every exigency,
endless endeavour to deserve their confidence.
Then there arises in regiments that mysterious
power which is called *esprit de corps*, when every
soul in them from the colonel to the drummer feels
that his own honour is bound up with the honour
of the regiment, and that the honour of the regiment
is the greatest thing in the world. And so you
find—for one instance out of many thousand—
such a battalion as that of the Fifty-seventh at
Albuera, with two men in every three struck down,
yet conscious of nothing in the dense smoke but of
closing in to the colours and unquestioning resolution
to die where they stood, rather than give way. So
too you find a simple solitary private, in the story
that I have already told you, content to go down
alone in a sinking ship for the honour of the Sixtieth.
Without knowledge of military history men are really
unconscious of the existence of that most wonderful
of moral forces, *esprit de corps* ; and it is not a thing
of which anyone can afford to be ignorant.

Lastly military history gives us insight into
the character and intellectual powers of some of
the most remarkable men who ever lived. I shall

be told perhaps that the career of an Alexander or
of a Caesar is but a paltry study compared with
that of a Luther or a François Xavier. Be it so.
Different characters attract different students, and
great leaders of men, whether saints or soldiers,
are always worthy of study. Moreover, it is a
most important thing to realise that military history
means the survey of administrative in at least as
great a degree as strategical and tactical genius.
You will all of you recall the happy phrase that
was applied to Carnot—the organiser of victory ;
and Carnot was only one of many who have deserved
the epithet.   No man perhaps ever merited it better
than Moses, if only through his standing order
(which you will find in the book of Deuteronomy
xxiii. 12–14) that when an army was in the field
there should be appointed places for latrines outside the camp, and that all foul matter should be
instantly buried. The regulation is justified by a
noble precept, which in its essence is true for all
time.   " The Lord thy God walketh in the midst
of thy camp to deliver thee and to give up thine
enemies before thee ; therefore *shall thy camp be
holy*, that he see no unclean thing in thee and turn
away from thee." Foul camps mean enteric fever
and dysentery, and these diseases mean the destruction of the host. To this day it may be said that
the sanitary regulations of Moses have never been

superseded. How many Jewish victories may have
been due to the observance of them we can only
conjecture ; how many hundred millions of lives
have been sacrificed to the neglect of them—for
it is only latterly that their value has been fully
recognised—the Omniscient alone can know.

Turn from Palestine to Greece and look at the
military constitution of Sparta founded by Lycurgus.
Make a huge stride over the ages, and look at Chaka,
the man of genius whose military organisation and
training of his people would have made the Zulus
masters of South Africa, had not the boundless
resources of the British Empire dashed his work—
though not without difficulty and defeat—at last
to the ground. Look at the great men of modern
times, whose names will be more familiar to you,
Frederick the Great, Napoleon, Wellington, and
take note that from the very beginning of history
the greatest generals have almost invariably been
in the very first rank not merely of military but of
civil administrators. It may seem heretical to say
so, but I personally am inclined to think that
Napoleon's work as a civil Governor transcends
even in its own kind the greatest of his military
achievements. I, even as many other men, have
gone through most of the thirty-six volumes of his
correspondence ; and I confess that his reorganisa-
tion of France in the first months of the Consulate—

crude and hasty as in many respects it was, owing
to the urgency of the case and the desperate nature
of the circumstances—appears to me the greatest
thing that ever he did. But all three of these men
are remarkable chiefly for the astonishing results
which they achieved with small means. Frederick,
in spite of terrible defeats and latterly an almost
total failure of resources, contrived somehow to
carry the Seven Years War to a successful end, and
at its close to revive an exhausted Prussia. Napoleon took over a France demoralised by ten years
of misrule, and sunk financially to a hopeless depth
of bankruptcy, yet by squandering men in lieu of
money he carried his eagles victoriously from end
to end of Europe. Wellington had so few men that
he could not squander them, and so little money
that, owing to the general lack of specie, he was
obliged to carry on the Peninsular War upon credit,
and incidentally to administer the government of
Portugal as well as direct the operations in the
field, lest that credit should absolutely fail him.
Yet by sheer administrative ability, patience and
tenacity, he prevailed.

I have of design left the question of the technical
study of strategy and tactics until the last. Strategy
may, I think, be defined as the art of bringing armies
up to the battle-field by the right way, in the right
strength, at the right time ; tactics as the art of

handling them on the battle-field to the best advantage. Of what profit is the study of these two arts to the citizen at large ? Well, in the first place he will learn what may be termed his strategical geography, and why battles are constantly fought century after century in or about the same places. He will understand why, for instance, endless great actions for the mastery of India have been fought within fifty miles of Delhi ; the significance of Stirling on the map of Scotland, and of Acre on the coast of Syria. He will perceive why, owing to changes in transport and armament, places whose names constantly occur in old diplomatic records have ceased to be of great account and are now seldom mentioned, whereas others, as I have said, retain their importance through endless generations. He will realise, further, how far strategic considerations enter into political arrangements of all kinds, as for instance that Bismarck the civilian was against the annexation of Alsace and Lorraine as tending to perpetuate the hostility of France, but was overruled by Moltke because the new frontier was worth 100,000 men. In fact it is not too much to say that knowledge of military history is essential to the right understanding not only of domestic and foreign politics, but of the whole story, written and unwritten, of the human race—which is mainly a story of fighting.

The interest of tactics is chiefly for professional men ; but it is worth while to notice its main principles, which are simple. All fighting is, and has always been, of two kinds, hand-to-hand or shock action, at a distance or missile action. Goliath challenged the Israelites to shock action, and David killed him by missile action ; and I dare say that the Philistines thought it unfair. Now, whether for shock or for missile action, it is very obvious that if you can overmatch your enemy in numbers—other things being equal—you are likely to get the better of him ; and that if you are on higher ground than he is you can see him better than he can see you to throw things at him, and can charge him with greater impetus down hill than he can meet you with, uphill. It may be said broadly that the art of tactics is the art of bringing stronger numbers to bear at some given point, and taking or acquiring superiority of position. This is the physical side of tactics. The moral side (apart from discipline) lies chiefly in those two eternal and undying resources, known as the ambush and the surprise. Here the leader tries to upset an enemy's physical advantage of numbers and position by taking him unawares. There is no finer example of a surprise in the world than that of Gideon. Think of it— the silent march of 300 picked men in three companies through the darkness, each with his trumpet

and his torch hidden in a pitcher, the silent sur-
rounding of the hostile camp just before dawn,
when human vitality is at its lowest ; and then the
silence broken by the crash of three hundred pitchers,
the sudden flare of the torches, the braying of three
hundred trumpets as if in signal to a host of thousands unseen in the night ; and the simultaneous
yell " For the Lord and for Gideon." There was
a wild panic in the Midianite camp, and no wonder.
In the darkness they took to fighting each other,
" every man's sword against his fellow." Of course
they did. Exactly the same result was seen many
times over during our last war in South Africa, and
has been seen in every panic from Gideon's age to
our own. Gideon was a man who studied moral
force.

Thus we come back to the point from which
we began. Military history is not the history of
physical but of moral force, perhaps almost of the
triumph of moral over purely physical force. Let
no man say that such a subject is unworthy of our
attention. It is unfortunately impossible to study
deeply any department of the affairs of men without
encountering much that is infinitely vile and base
and sordid ; and military history is no exception
to this rule. But it is rich also in noble and heroic
deeds, not of valour only but of patience, self-
sacrifice and endurance. I may be wrong, but I

think that I see in it grander and more frequent examples of devotion to duty than in any other branch of history. The opportunities, you will say, are greater ; and there may be some truth in this ; but I would add that the training to self-abnegation counts also for very much. It will harm none of us to know well this story of duty done for duty's sake ; and it may be that, as the example of the *Birkenhead* has nerved all our race to face with calmness the utmost perils of the sea, so the remembrance of the proud history of our soldiers may brace each one of us, no matter how humble his sphere, to discipline himself in the self-denial and self-control which triumph over adversity.

LECTURE II

BRITISH MILITARY HISTORY

In my last lecture I attempted to deal with the broad subject of military history at large. To-day I shall treat of the narrower subject of British military history. There is nothing arbitrary or capricious in this ; for British military history is, owing to our insular position, a thing apart.

Foreign nations, indeed, would say that a country which has never in the whole course of her existence put fifty thousand of her own children in line upon any battle-field and very rarely so many even as thirty thousand, can have no military history ; but none the less we have one, which is in many ways remarkable and worthy of study.

Note in the first place that for five hundred years after the Conquest England was not a purely insular power. She had troublesome neighbours in Wales and Scotland, and her kings had possessions, and consequently troublesome neighbours, in France. Remember that it was not until 1558 that we lost Calais, and that, as long as we possessed it, we had so to speak a bridge-head which enabled us to enter France practically at any moment. This was a sad temptation towards foolish expeditions and waste of strength ; and it was a great blessing to us really when the capture of Calais removed it for ever.

Elizabeth, therefore, was our first purely insular sovereign. What manner of military force did she find at her accession, and what manner of organisation for creating and maintaining it ? The sovereign was empowered, as he still is, to call out every able-bodied man for the defence of the country ; and upon the different classes of freemen was imposed by an Act of 1558, which was based upon an older Act of 1285, the duty of providing themselves with arms according to their means. Long before 1558 fire-arms had been brought to such efficiency that a complete system of tactics had been founded for their use by the ablest soldiers on the Continent ;

but in England the Statute still professed content-
ment with the weapons of three centuries earlier,
bows and bills ; and there were remarkably few fire-
arms in the country at all. There were, however,
great traditions derived in part from Saxon times,
but strengthened, developed and enlarged by the
victories of Edward the Third, his son Edward,
Prince of Wales, and king Harry the Fifth, in France
and in Spain in the fourteenth and fifteenth
centuries.

I told you in my last lecture that all fighting,
from the earliest times to the present, is in the
ultimate resort of two kinds—hand-to-hand or shock
action, at a distance or missile action. In the hands
of the English a very old missile weapon, the bow,
had become, in the form of the long bow, the most
deadly and formidable of its time. Every English
boy was trained to the use of it, and was taught to
bring every muscle of his body to bear upon it, just
as in rowing you are taught not to row with your
arms only, but with your legs also and with all the
weight of your body. "My father taught me to lay
my body to the bow," says Bishop Hugh Latimer.
The result was that their arrows were discharged
with great rapidity and accuracy, and with such
strength that they were effective in the matter of
penetration at an astonishingly long range. The
shock action of mediaeval times, as you know,

was confined chiefly to mounted men-at-arms, clad in armour from head to foot, and furnished with lances, who moved in dense masses at very moderate speed, and trampled down everything that stood in their way. How did the English archers deal with them ? They aimed mainly at their horses, which, maddened by the pain, ran away with their riders, and carried confusion everywhere ; but being accurate shots, the archers aimed also at the joints of the harness—at the intervals between gorget and breast-plate, between breast-plate, or back-plate, and thigh-pieces, which were exposed by the swaying of the body, and above all the arm-pit when the arm was raised to strike. But how about the English men-at-arms, you will ask ? Why did not the enemy shoot their horses with arrows, and make them unmanageable also ? Here we come to the English peculiarity. The English men-at-arms always dismounted to fight, broke off their lances to a length that could be easily handled and, ranked together in a dense mass, used them as pikes. So here there was the tradition of a missile infantry, so to speak, steady and deadly shots ; and of a shock infantry which could not be broken and, moreover, after winning a victory could mount and pursue on horseback.

The new tactics of the Continent, which the English had to learn, had taken much the same

direction. The Swiss, in order to keep mounted
men-at-arms at a distance, had bethought them
of ranging their infantry into dense masses, arm'ed
with pikes fourteen feet long, and this they had done
with such success that they had vindicated the
position of infantry as the most important element
on the battle-field.   Other nations took up the idea,
either for mercenaries or national troops; and,
with the improvement of fire-arms, missile infantry
developed into musketeers, or " shot " as they were
called, who fought entirely as skirmishers, while shock
infantry was represented by dense masses of pikemen.
Simultaneously the cavalry became a missile force.
Unable to make any impression against a bristling
wall of pikes, they gave up their lances and provided
themselves with pistols, so as to shoot the pikemen
down from a distance.   Hence it was customary
to cover the pikemen with heavy armour on breast
and thighs, which prevented them from moving very
fast. The fate of the battle, however, was determined
by them. Musketeers and cavaliers worried each
other and the pikemen for as long as they dared,
but the ultimate issue was decided when pike met
pike. The chief reason for this was the system
adopted for maintaining a continuous fire. This
was to range the musketeers in ten ranks, and let
these ranks fire in succession, the first rank filing to
the rear as soon as its weapons were discharged, in

order to reload, and leaving the second rank to do likewise, and so on. In theory the system was ingenious; but in practice it was found that men thought a great deal more about filing to the rear rapidly, than about firing steadily and accurately. Of course if heavy artillery could be brought within range of a square of pikemen, it might blast them off the field; but cannon were too cumbrous and difficult to move for this to be often possible; and thus the decision of the day was left, as it still is, to cold steel. You will see wonderful pictures of combats of pikemen, just as you see the like representations of fights with the bayonet. I doubt greatly if they ever occurred. Both sides approached each other with the pike or bayonet no doubt; but before they closed one side turned and ran away. All nations boast of their prowess with the bayonet, our own among others, but few men really enjoy a hand-to-hand fight with the bayonet, however much they may enjoy a hand-to-hand pursuit. You remember that the Homeric heroes, after a certain amount of close combat, invariably threw stones at each other; and the practice has never died out. English and French both talk much of the bayonet; but in Egypt in 1801 they threw stones at each other when their ammunition was exhausted, and one English sergeant was killed by a stone. At Inkerman again the British threw stones at the Russians, not

without effect ; and I am told upon good authority
that the Russians and Japanese, both of whom
profess to love the bayonet, threw stones at each
other, rather than close, even in this twentieth
century.

To this stage, then, had the art of war advanced
at Elizabeth's accession, but no effort was made to
train the national forces according to the latest
methods.   A few foreign mercenaries were imported
from time to time, and a great many English went
abroad, and served either in the armies of Spain—
which were the most efficient of their day—or in
those of the revolted Dutch which, under the Princes
of the House of Nassau, were rapidly improving upon
the Spanish methods.   Thus some ideas of foreign
practice crept into England, and a great deal of
foreign nomenclature, which still remains with us.
Nearly all of our military terms are foreign, drawn
mostly from the French, the Italian or the Spanish.
Regiment, battalion, colonel, sergeant-major, captain,
lieutenant, ensign, cornet, corporal, centinel—all
are words borrowed from Latin sources, and one
could multiply the number of instances.   Pistol and
howitzer are Bohemian, relics of John Zizka.   For-
lorn hope (which has nothing to do with the English
word *hope*) is Dutch.   Even Shakespeare speaks
twice of recruits by the Spanish name *bisoño*,
corrupted into Bezonian.

Little progress was made in Elizabeth's time, and no more in the reign of James I ; but meanwhile a great military reformer arose in the person of Gustavus Adolphus of Sweden, who recognised that missile action was that which must triumph in the future, and set himself to·improve the firing tactics of infantry. This he did by reducing the depth of the infantry to three ranks, and forming the musketeers shoulder to shoulder, the front rank kneeling. He then distributed the whole of his battalions into sections, or platoons, of twenty to thirty men each, and introduced the system of firing by volleys of platoons ; the usual method being that the first, third, fifth, seventh and ninth platoons fired first in rapid succession, and then the second, fourth, sixth, eighth and tenth, by which time the odd-numbered platoons had reloaded and were prepared to begin again. Thus a continuous fire was maintained without unsteadiness or disorder ; and the system was so good that it lasted until the introduction of breech-loaders. There being many Scots—even whole regiments—and a good many English in the Swedish service, the drill and tactics of Gustavus became known to a number of people in both kingdoms.

Now followed the Civil War, wherein the armies on both sides were ridiculously inefficient until Cromwell, recognising that the King had most of the gentlemen—that is to say the more efficient amateurs—upon his side, decided that he must train professional soldiers to beat them. So he raised his famous regiment of horse, and for the first time since the days of Harry the Fifth brought true military discipline to bear upon English soldiers. In 1645 the Parliament perceived that a whole army trained upon the new principle would mean the difference between triumph and defeat, and thereupon organised the famous host called the New Model Army, consisting of twelve regiments of foot, eleven regiments of horse and a train of artillery. The effect was immediate. The Royalist cause was utterly overthrown, whether upheld by English, Scots or Irish ; the irresistible army displaced the Long Parliament and took from it its usurped authority ; and Cromwell during five years of unrest and uneasiness kept the peace in the three kingdoms by means of regular troops and an armed constabulary. Never before or since have we been kept in such order. Scottish Highlanders, Irish Tories, English colliers—as lawless a people as the other two—were hammered and cowed into obedience. Some north-country colliers attempted a strike ; " they would neither work themselves nor suffer others," said the newspapers. The Lord Protector sent a regiment of horse to the spot, and nothing more was heard of the strike. Nor was it only within

the British Isles that he was feared, for, in virtue of
his army, he was dreaded throughout Europe. His
reign was brief, but he contrived within his five short
years to strike a fatal blow at Dutch commercial
supremacy, to ensure by his regulations as to trade
and navigation that it should pass to England, and
to call representatives from an United Kingdom to
a single Assembly at Westminster.

And now pause for a moment to look at the
portentous changes that had come over England in
the hundred years between the accession of Elizabeth
in 1558 and the death of Cromwell in 1658. In the
first place England, as I have said, had been finally
cut off from the Continent ; in the second she had
become mistress in her own house, for, though
Scotland was not administratively joined to her,
the two crowns had been united upon one head and
closer union was only a question of time ; while
Ireland had been subjected to so stern a discipline
that she still chafes at the remembrance of it. Insular therefore the British Isles were as never before
in their history ; and yet in the earlier half of the
seventeenth century there had been laid by private
adventurers under Royal Charter the foundations of
a colonial empire in North America and the West
Indies, that is to say in the temperate and in the
torrid zone, as also of a great agency for foreign trade
in India. Moreover Britain's powerful neighbour,

France, had almost simultaneously formed settlements or trading establishments precisely in the three same quarters. Almost at the instant therefore when the British were relieved of the perils and anxieties of a land frontier at home, they began to acquire such a frontier over seas. Lastly they had evolved, in what may be called its perfected state, a scheme of commercial policy which was not likely to make for peace with their neighbours. Meanwhile, owing to the accidental circumstance of a civil war and the happy advent of a man of genius, they had produced quite casually the very thing that was needed for the new conditions, a regular army subject to proper military discipline.

When Charles II was restored, the intention was to disband the entire army of the Commonwealth, or to keep at most a regiment of foot-guards, which had fought against the forces of the Commonwealth in Flanders, and a regiment of horse-guards, composed of Royalist gentlemen. But as these showed themselves inefficient in dealing with the London mob, two of the Parliamentary regiments were also retained, Monk's of infantry—now the Coldstream Guards—and a composite body of horse, which we now know as the Blues. This sufficed for domestic police ; but soon there arose the question of colonial garrisons, for Katharine of Bragança, Queen of Charles II, had brought to him as a dowry Tangier and Bombay ; and there were other places, notably New York and St Kitts, where the close neighbour-hood of the French made a little protection very desirable. How were these to be provided ? It was a time-honoured custom in England that all fortified places should have a small permanent garrison indissolubly attached to them, rather to keep the buildings in order than to provide for their defence ; and this custom was now extended. A few com-panies were raised for New York and St Kitts, and two regiments of foot and one of dragoons for Tangier ; but even so it was necessary to send the Guards abroad from London to quell a rebellion in Virginia, and to give further assistance at Tangier. In India the East India Company pursued the same policy, keeping some companies of white troops at Bombay and Madras, and forming also companies of natives, the number of which was constantly increased, for defence of their factories.

James II who succeeded his brother in 1685 was a trained soldier and sailor who had seen much active service, and an admirable departmental adminis-trator. He made a pretext of Monmouth's rebellion to augment the standing army considerably; and, if more time had been given to him, he would probably have established an efficient War Office and laid the foundations of a sound military system. Further, noticing the danger to the American colonies from their constant divisions and quarrels in the presence of the smaller but perfectly united and organised French settlements, he remodelled the governments of many of them, grouping them together under English Governors, who were also soldiers, so that in time of danger there might be harmonious action and efficient defence. These changes, principally, cost him his throne.

During all these years the English had never ceased to chafe at the continued existence of a standing army. The country gentlemen, who had made the Revolution of 1642, had the terror of Oliver Cromwell before their eyes, and dreaded lest the Stuarts might emulate his summary and efficient methods. They professed, some of them no doubt conscientiously, solicitude for the liberties of England, forgetting that their forerunners of the Long Parliament had abolished the Monarchy and the House of Lords and erected themselves into a permanent committee of tyrants. ' They protested that a standing army was unknown to the Constitution of England, but they had not awaked to the fact that there was a British Empire in the making, and that such an Empire requires police. They could not, or at any rate did not, look one inch before their noses except at one principal object, namely the supplanting of the monarchy, in substance if not in fact, by an oligarchy of their noble selves. They therefore encouraged sedition and discontent with the new arrangements in the colonies, and invited William of Orange to come with an armed force and accept the Crown from them. It suited William's policy exactly to have in his hands the resources of England for his desperate struggle against France; and he came, bringing with him the certainty of a great war.

It has been my fate to study the departmental administration of England at various periods, but I have never found it quite so corrupt and inefficient as in the early years of King William's reign. James had improved it amazingly in his three years of power; but his men were of course displaced in favour of the Whig magnates and their nominees, naturally with bad results. The administrative reforms of James in the American colonies were likewise upset by the Revolution; and this folly brought us within measurable distance of the loss of North America, besides taking the resources of England to defend people who ought to have been able to defend themselves. However there the matter was. It was necessary to raise a number of regiments and improvise an army for the pacification of Ireland, which was, I think, the very worst force ever put together under the English flag. After many disgraceful episodes Ireland was re-conquered; and then the army, which was by this

time beginning to improve, was transported over to
Flanders for operations there. It fought in many
severe actions with credit but mostly without
success, for William III was not a great general.
However, it learned a great deal, particularly in the
matter of sieges, of which it had known very little,
and being thrown into company with some good
troops and into opposition against others, it was
roused to emulation of the high standard of
French and Dutch efficiency.   In 1697 the war
came to an end through the exhaustion of both
parties.

Of the solid improvements effected by the
incidents of this war, the first was the passing of
the Mutiny Act, in consequence of the mutiny of a
regiment which was faithful to King James. This
Act empowered the king to punish military crimes,
for which the civil law provided no penalty. A
standing army being unknown to the Constitution
of England, the Act was passed for twelve months
only, a ridiculous piece of pedantry which is still
perpetuated in the Annual Army Act. The next
reform was the adoption of the bayonet, a recent
invention, which united the pike and the musket
into a single weapon, and made an end of the
distinction between shock infantry and missile
infantry. A third was the gradual disuse of the
pistol by cavalry ; the discarding more and more of

its defensive armour and the reversion to shock action by the charge at high speed.

Immediately upon the conclusion of the peace there was a howl in the Commons for the reduction of the Army ; and it was carried that the English establishment should be fixed at no more than seven thousand men, though the much poorer island of Ireland had been permanently charged by an earlier act with an establishment of twelve thousand. I must explain that until 1708 there were three separate military establishments for England, Scotland and Ireland, and after 1708 two for Great Britain and Ireland until the Act of Union in 1800. Moreover, you must remember that even within the memory of living men the infantry and cavalry were under the War Office, the artillery and engineers under the Office of Ordnance, and the commissariat and transport under the Treasury, so that, while the three kingdoms were disunited, there were nine offices concerned with the administration of the Army ; and the colonels, who were responsible for the clothing, made a tenth authority. Hence it was no easy task to get the Army under way for any duty; while the creation of any new force was a most bewildering labour. The Commons, however, cared for none of these things. France was evidently only taking breath for another spring ; but that they ignored, and, as I have said, cut down the Army to

the ridiculous figure of nineteen thousand men.
William very nearly abdicated the throne of England
in disgust at their conduct.

Here then we must notice the first flagrant
instance of a besetting sin, which, practically from
the very beginning up to the present time, has
afflicted and still afflicts the House of Commons.
No sooner is the country at peace than it raises a
cry for the reduction of the Army. In the eighteenth
century this cry was very much a matter of faction.
The Whigs had always bitterly opposed a standing
army under the Stuarts, when they thought it adverse
to their interests ; and the Tories naturally conceived a mortal detestation of it after it had become
a weapon in the hands of the Whigs. Thus both
parties were committed to general discouragement
of the force ; and any member who desired to pose
as a champion of liberty could do so effectively by
denouncing the evils of a standing army. It has
been my hard fate to wade through a prodigious
number of speeches upon this subject, and I have
been absolutely nauseated by their hollowness and
cant. It is of course possible for a man to object
sincerely and conscientiously to any description of
army ; but I have never met with such a one in the
Parliamentary debates of the eighteenth century.
Their abuse of standing armies, in which was generally
mixed some vituperation of the military profession

at large, was simply hypocrisy and cant, most mischievous and dangerous, inasmuch as it brought the calling of a soldier into contempt, and kindled the entire civil population into hostility with the military.

Compelled to reduce the Army to a mere handful of men, William sought to turn this handful to the best account by keeping the skeletons of a great many regiments, which might on emergency be filled out with additional men, rather than a very few complete regiments ready to take the field at once. He was quite right; and his example has repeatedly been followed down to our own days; but the system of skeleton regiments means always unreadiness for war. In the haste and urgency of the first hostilities all the trained men are swept into a few battalions, so as to fill up their empty ranks; those few battalions are sent into action; in six months they are so much reduced by losses as to be ineffective; and you are left with nothing but recruits who need two or three years to convert them into soldiers. This has happened again and again, and the first instance of it came in 1701. In November 1700 the acceptance of the throne of Spain for his grandson by Louis XIV roused all Europe to arms; and Louis to secure his object invaded Spanish Flanders, surrounded several towns which were occupied, under the Treaty of 1697, by Dutch troops, and so cut off fifteen thousand of William's best men. Under a former treaty of alliance with Holland England was bound to furnish to her ten thousand men, and both Houses of Parliament prepared faithfully to fulfil the obligation. Twelve battalions were accordingly ordered to the Low Countries from Ireland, eked out of course by a great many young soldiers, but with a fair leaven of old ones; and the country flattered itself that it would escape with no further burden. But, as usual, Parliament had forgotten the Empire. Bad news came just at the same moment from the West Indies, and it was imperative to send two thousand more men to that quarter. Thus at one fell swoop the garrison of Ireland was snatched away, and it was necessary to raise at once ten thousand new recruits and four new battalions. Before the end of the year Louis XIV recognised the son of James II as King of England; and Parliament, at last roused to indignation, agreed to furnish a contingent of forty thousand men—eighteen thousand British, and the rest foreigners. Thereupon orders were issued for the raising of fifteen more new regiments, at enormous expense; for, in consequence of the ill-treatment of the army by Parliament at the close of the last war, men could not be tempted to enlist except by large bounties. In 1703 the English share in the contest extended to the Spanish Peninsula, and

eight new regiments were raised for the purpose. In
1704 the capture of Gibraltar and other operations
demanded the levying of six more regiments ; in
1706 thirteen new regiments were added ; and to
make a long story short, before the war ended in
1713 sixty-nine new corps of horse and foot had been
formed to carry on the war.

But we must not leave that war without a sketch
of the greatest of English generals who conducted
it. John Churchill was born, you remember, in
1650, received his first commission in the Guards in
1667, saw active service against the Moors in Tangier
a year or two later, and serious warfare in 1672
against the United Provinces under Condé, Turenne
and Luxemburg, continuing to serve them under the
colours of Louis XIV, as was not uncommon at the
time, until 1677. In the course of those five years
he learned his work under the great master Turenne,
while fighting another great master, Montecuculi.
In 1689 he commanded a small contingent of
British troops against the French once more in
Flanders ; besides which, saving a little work in
Ireland, he was employed no more by William
until 1698 ; being suspected, I fear with justice, of
treasonable relations with the exiled King James II.
Finally in 1702 he was appointed to the command
of the Allied Forces in the Low Countries, thus
finding himself for the first time a general-in-chief

at the age of fifty-two. In those days of bad roads there were few districts where armies could keep the field, owing to the difficulty of feeding them ; for a campaign, as I told you in my first lecture, is a picnic. The delta of the Rhine and Meuse was a cock-pit because it was in the first place rich in food, and in the second traversed by navigable rivers and canals, which made the transport of victuals, of heavy guns, and of ammunition comparatively easy. But being a cock-pit, its waterways were studded with innumerable fortresses, constructed to prevent ingress into France from the north, and into what we now call Belgium but which in Marlborough's time was known as the Austrian Netherlands, from the south. Hence it naturally followed that a war in that quarter signified a war of sieges ; and the French Court was fond of sieges, because it could attend them in state and take charge of the operations with much glory and little discomfort or danger. It must be added that incessant warfare in that unfortunate country had made every feature in it so familiar, that the ordinary tactical and strategical movements in it were as well known as the moves on a chess-board.

It was a mark of Marlborough's originality of mind that on this familiar ground he contrived always to do something unexpected. Had he not been hampered by disloyal Dutch Generals and

timid Dutch deputies, who controlled the Dutch
contingent of his army and therefore the Commander-in-Chief also, he would have driven the
French out of Flanders in two campaigns. As it
was, these so-called allies deliberately foiled him
again and again; and, since the French arms had
been uniformly successful against the Imperial
troops on the Upper Rhine and Danube, the way
to Vienna was by the year 1704 practically open
to the French armies. Then it was that Marlborough, seeing that the case was desperate, conceived the magnificent idea of a march of some
three hundred miles from the Low Countries to
join the Imperial army on the Danube. The
difficulties were immense. In the first place he
had to gain permission from numbers of petty
princes to pass through their territory; in the
second he had to provide magazines of food and
clothing for his army all along the line of march,
as well as money to pay them with; and all this
he had to do with secrecy and circumspection for,
in the third place, it was essential that the French
armies should gain no inkling of his intentions,
but should be absolutely deceived by his movements
until he was so far advanced upon his way that he
could not be caught. It seems impossible that
such a thing could have been done; but done it
was; and the two victories of the Schellenberg

and of Blenheim were the result. Moreover, this campaign, though the most celebrated because of its extreme originality and boldness, by no means stands alone as an example of Marlborough's surpassing skill in the field. You may go through the whole of the campaigns that he fought in Flanders, ten in all; and in every one you will find some salient feature which betrays the master. The forcing of the French lines on the Geete in 1705; the feint which beguiled Vendôme into a fatal blunder at Ramillies in 1706; the wonderful march before Oudenarde in 1708; the investment of Tournay in 1709; the amazing wiles by which he turned the lines of La Bassée in 1711—any one of these achievements would suffice to make the fortune of an ordinary general.

What then were the qualities which made Marlborough so astonishingly successful in the field—and not in the field only—for you must remember that he was no less great as a diplomatist than as a general? First I should say what Wellington termed his strong cool common-sense. This sounds perhaps a small matter to you; but what after all is common-sense? It is above all the faculty of seeing things as they are, and of framing your action accordingly. The faculty of seeing things as they are, swift, true and penetrating insight into the heart of things, undistracted

by their outward semblance—this, whether it be
the attribute of statesman, general, poet or painter,
is genius. And to frame your actions, as a man
of action, upon real insight, what does that mean ?
It means transcendent moral courage, the courage
of faith in one's own judgement, the courage to
depart from beaten tracks, the courage to brave
the disapprobation of those who cannot do without
such tracks, the courage, in a good sense, to take
liberties. It is the union of courage with insight
which makes a man original. And there was
another form of genius which Marlborough possessed in a supreme degree, the faculty of taking
infinite pains. When his army started for the
Danube not a man knew whither he was bound ;
yet at every stage food was ready for all, and at
certain points shoes to replace those worn out on
the march, and money to provide the troops with
pay. For, as Marlborough well knew, soldiers
who have not what they need will help themselves,
and plunder means indiscipline, and indiscipline
turns an army into a rabble. Any officer can flog
and shoot and punish, and say that he enforces
discipline ; but a good officer prefers to enforce it
by removing all temptation to indiscipline. Next,
Marlborough possessed in a transcendent degree
the divine gift of patience—patience which
conquers all things. His temper was almost

miraculously placid and calm. Time after time
the Dutch deputies thwarted his shrewdest strokes
and most brilliant combinations ; and time after
time he endured their maddening mischief without
a murmur, without even a semblance of displeasure,
waiting for better times, and preferring to bear
almost any mortification rather than endanger
the common cause. There are few things greater
in Marlborough than this. " I would not have
that man's temper for the world," he is reported
to have remarked when watching a groom who was
fighting his horse in the saddle. So strongly
marked was this characteristic that when once,
in order to deceive his enemy, he grew from day
to day more cantankerous and pretended at last
to lose all self-control, his army declared sorrow-
fully that Corporal John had lost his wits. And
this epithet—Corporal John—brings me to the last
great gift of Marlborough, his extraordinary personal
charm. It nowhere appears that he laid himself
out particularly to attract his fellow-creatures ;
but not one of them could resist him. His men
adored him. It was not only that he enjoyed their
confidence as a successful leader ; but that he
commanded their affection. And others shared
this feeling as strongly as the soldiers. In 1705
he narrowly escaped capture by a marauding party
of French. On his arrival at the Hague after the

incident the whole population, high and low, turned out to welcome him, the poor crowding round him with tears of joy and kissing even his horse and his boots. Of course there is a dark side to his character, and much has been made of his avarice and his treachery. But I have noticed that men who begin with nothing and rise to great estate, as did Marlborough, are apt to be careful of sixpences to the very end ; and I do not know that it is to their discredit. It is certain too that he declined even to look at an enormous bribe offered by Louis XIV to obtain an advantageous peace. Moreover, you will find that at all times and in all countries while the issue of a struggle between two dynasties is still doubtful, men tend to keep upon friendly terms with both. I do not say that this trait is a beautiful or an honourable one ; but that it is the rule and not the exception is beyond doubt ; and we must take poor human nature as we find it. Fortunate are we when we find this weakness redeemed by such great qualities as were possessed by Marlborough.

The Peace of Utrecht which brought the war to an end was, as you remember, the work of the Tories, who had succeeded in ousting the Whigs and disgracing Marlborough. Before the Treaty had been signed, they had reduced the British establishment to twenty-two thousand men ; and,

when the Whigs returned to power upon the accession of George I in 1714, they continued the evil
work which the Tories had begun. By 1719 the
establishment had been reduced to twelve thousand
men, making with the same number in Ireland a
nominal total of twenty-four thousand. Yet the
Treaty had added to the Empire Gibraltar, Minorca,
Nova Scotia and Newfoundland, all of which required
garrisons ; there was no police in the British Isles ;
the organisation of the Militia was so antiquated
that the force was absolutely useless ; and there
was always danger, as the country experienced in
1715, of a Jacobite rising in Scotland. Moreover,
the original system of defence in the West Indies
was rapidly becoming obsolete ; and it was pretty
evident that the burden must shortly be trans-
ferred to the Imperial forces. No consideration
could move the British Parliament to accept the
Army as a necessary institution. Walpole in 1722
at last insisted that the British Establishment
should be raised permanently to eighteen thousand
men ; but even so it would have been impossible
to collect ten thousand for any emergency without
leaving the royal palaces and strong places un-
guarded. Yet Parliament, not content with
keeping an inadequate army, insisted also that it
should be inefficient. In Ireland, from want of
billeting accommodation, barracks had been built

for the troops ; but nothing could persuade Parliament to extend the same system to England. No ! the regiments must be broken up and scattered among ale-houses, "in order that the people might feel the burden that lay upon them." Moreover, hon. members conceived that ale-houses grew as abundantly at Gibraltar, Nova Scotia and Newfoundland as in England ; and could hardly be brought to house the garrisons of these places adequately. Scores of men died in all these spots from exposure—and why ? Because the nation had laid itself in bondage to a canting phrase. This ill-treatment of the soldiers, joined to perpetual reviling of the military profession, of course made the Army unpopular. Men were unwilling to enlist and very ready to desert, which led in turn to high bounties to tempt recruits ; and this again led to fraudulent enlistment and hideous waste of money. Of all the cant that ever was canted in this canting world none is so cantful as the assertion that neglect of military precaution is economy. Yet the British people after two centuries' experience of its falsehood still hugs the notion passionately to its bosom.

The peace was broken in 1739 by a sudden outburst of national cupidity for the wealth of Spain ; but from this point, where the struggle for Empire becomes acute, I shall in this lecture

confine myself to our wars in Europe only, leaving
those in the Colonies and in India for two future
lectures. Before the quarrel with Spain was fairly
ended, we found ourselves entangled in the War
of the Austrian Succession, with an obligation to
furnish sixteen thousand men to uphold the cause
of Maria Theresa. British and French, by a curious
fiction, were engaged at the outset only as auxiliaries upon either side; and they actually fought
the battle of Dettingen before war had been formally
declared between them. From the spring of 1744,
however, they met as principals and, since the
French had been triumphantly driven from Germany at the end of 1743, on the familiar ground of
the Austrian Netherlands. The British contingent
was increased from sixteen thousand men in 1743 to
twenty-five thousand in 1745, the balance of the
force being composed of Dutch and Austrians;
but this strength in the field, trifling though it was,
was only attained by reducing the garrisons of Great
Britain to fifteen thousand men, mostly raw recruits.
The Duke of Cumberland on the 11th of May, 1745,
fought and lost a murderous battle at Fontenoy;
and in July there came the astounding news that
Prince Charles Edward had landed in Scotland and
was gathering the Highland clans about him. In
the whole of North Britain there were only three
thousand untrained men who wore the red coat;

and bold action combined with good fortune on the part of Prince Charles soon filled these with the spirit of panic. Within little more than two months he was at Edinburgh and, but for the garrisons of the Castle of Stirling and one or two lesser strongholds, master of the country. Urgent messengers were sent to Cumberland in Flanders for reinforcements; and not English troops only, but Dutch and Hessians, were hurried across the German Ocean to save the throne of the Guelphs. There was every reason to dread lest the remnant of the army in Flanders, reduced to utter weakness by the loss of these detachments, should be overwhelmed by the French; but fortunately the enemy took no advantage of their opportunity. Meanwhile Charles by skilful manœuvring evaded the troops opposed to him and reached Derby; and there now seemed to be nothing to prevent him from entering London. Fearing, however, the closing in of the British forces in his rear, and hearing that French troops had landed at Montrose to join him, he retired once more to Scotland; nor was it until he had won two or three further small actions, that he was finally and hopelessly defeated at Culloden. By that time, though he had landed originally with but seven companions and had never commanded more than seven or eight thousand mostly undisciplined men, he had kept the bulk of the British Army

employed for over nine months, and had beaten
several detachments of it handsomely. The episode
is generally treated as a romantic adventure ; but
it is really one of the most discreditable to be found
in our history ; and it was due entirely to the fanatics,
both Whig and Tory, who were always clamouring
against a standing army.

After the defeat of the insurgents the war was
continued in the Low Countries, where the Allies
sustained two more defeats, until in 1748, owing to
the exhaustion of all parties, it was closed by the
Peace of Aix-la-Chapelle, leaving the French and
English at the end very much as they had been at
the beginning. In a way it might seem that the
British had been dragged into the contest mainly
on account of the Kingdom of Hanover, but, as
we shall see in a future lecture, the war resolved
itself into a continuation of the struggle with France
for the possession of the new world. That struggle
in fact never ceased over the seas, both east and
west, and early in 1756 it came to an issue in open
war. As usual England was unready. German
troops were actually imported for the defence of the
realm ; Minorca was taken by the French ; everything went wrong in America ; and the state of affairs
seemed to be desperate. At last a competent
Minister, William Pitt the elder, was raised to power
and from that moment things began to improve.

The foreign troops were sent back to Germany; their place was taken by Militia; and an immense levy of recruits was begun for the increase of the regular Army. In the year 1756 France, Austria, Russia and Sweden leagued themselves together to crush Frederick the Great; and Pitt, perceiving that America might be conquered in Germany, decided to send a contingent of British troops, together with Hanoverians and Hessians, to Frederick's assistance. Moreover, as we had no competent general of our own, he asked Frederick to provide one; and thus for the first time British troops were placed under the command of a foreign general for service on the Continent. Few people know anything of the campaigns of Ferdinand of Brunswick, though they are distinguished by two of the finest performances of the British soldier: of the infantry at Minden, and of the cavalry at Warburg. And the reason of this is that, as I have said, the expedition, so far as England was concerned, was a diversion to help her to the conquest of the Empire. That conquest proceeded apace during the years 1759 to 1762, and by the end of the latter year we had expelled the French from Canada, India and the West Indies, besides depriving the Spaniards of Havana and Manila. The process demanded a great number of troops, for seventy-five per cent. of the men in the West Indies died or were

incapacitated for further service, and it is here that
we strike the weak point of Pitt's military administration.

The great Minister saw the importance of re-
organising the Militia, though as a matter of fact
he never enforced his own scheme of passing all
able-bodied men through the ranks—or in other
words of instituting national service. But he
never matured nor even considered (so far as we
can discover) any sound scheme for maintaining
the voluntary army that was serving abroad. His
only plan was to name a certain sum for bounty,
and scatter broadcast commissions to any individuals
who would undertake to raise independent companies
or regiments. In this way the nominal strength of
the Army was brought up to one hundred and fifty
battalions of infantry and thirty-two of cavalry,
the numbered regiments of infantry being as many
as one hundred and twenty-four. Comparatively
few of these new regiments survived, because they
had been formed simply and solely to be broken
up immediately and drafted into other battalions.
But what did this mean ? It meant in the first
place that hundreds of officers went about the
country trying to make money out of the recruiting
business by obtaining recruits for less than the pre-
scribed bounty, and pocketing the difference. It
meant secondly that crimps arose by the score who

contracted to supply recruits to these officers, of
course at a considerable profit to themselves, and
that thus there were so to speak two middlemen
to be paid out of the bounty as well as the recruit.
The inevitable result was that the country paid
vast sums to obtain worn-out old men, half-witted
lads and weedy boys, who were absolutely useless
in the field, and served only to fill graves and hospitals. Moreover, it was saddled with the obligation
of giving half-pay to field-officers, captains and even
subalterns, who had gained their rank by the simple
process of a bargain with the crimps. Meanwhile
the recruits, being enlisted not for some old corps
with a regimental history and a regimental pride
of its own, but for some ephemeral battalion which
was dispersed as soon as formed, felt no sentiment
of honour in their calling and deserted right and
left. One consequence of this exceedingly wasteful
system was that the resources of England both in
money and men were exhausted before peace was
made, and that the war could not have been carried
on for another twelve months even if it had been
necessary. But yet more fatal than this was the
misfortune that the system, owing to its supposed
success, received consecration from the great name
of Pitt. In the bitter struggle with France which
began in 1793 and ended at Waterloo I have
said that France squandered men to save money,

and that England squandered money to save men.
The elder Pitt squandered both money and men.

The conclusion of peace in 1763 found England
in possession of Gibraltar and Minorca in Europe;
Bermuda, the Bahamas, several West Indian Islands
and practically the entire continent of North America
east of the Rocky Mountains from the mouth of the
St Lawrence in the north to the Lower Mississippi
in the south. I omit the name of India, for that
is a subject to be treated separately. The military
establishment of England and Ireland for the defence
of this vast Empire was fixed at about forty-five
thousand men, two-thirds of them roughly speaking
at home, and one-third abroad. This was neither
more nor less than madness ; yet nevertheless many
were found, so great a man as Burke among them,
to condemn the " huge increase " as they called it
of the Army. But this was not the worst. Prices
generally had risen and the pay of the soldier was
too small for his subsistence ; wherefore recruits
could hardly be obtained by any shift, and the ranks
of regiments were miserably empty. Reeling under
the burden of the debts bequeathed by the late war,
England proposed to the Colonies that they should
share that burden with her. The North American
provinces admitted the justice of the claim but
made no effort to meet it ; whereupon the British
Government, after exhausting all expedients for

obtaining a contribution from them, fell back upon the only possible solution of the problem—impartial taxation of all the Colonies by Act of the Imperial Parliament, with a special provision that every penny of the money so raised should be spent in the Colonies themselves. A faction in the Colonies raised a loud outcry over this ; and the question, owing to mismanagement in England and to the provocative violence of the American agitators, finally issued in war between Mother-country and Colonies.

The task of bringing America to submission by force of arms was a military operation beyond the strength of any nation in the world at that time, and very far beyond that of England as she was in 1775. No effort was made to augment the Army until hostilities had actually broken out, and consequently there were no troops at hand. Recruiting, moreover, was so difficult, owing to the insufficiency of the pay, that the country resorted to the hiring of German mercenaries and to the transfer of Hanoverian battalions to Gibraltar and Minorca, so as to release four British battalions from thence. Faction violently obstructed all military measures until a great disaster to our arms in 1777 made it practically certain that France would declare war ; but then, in spite of all the ravings of the King's enemies at home, patriotic feeling prevailed, and

fifteen thousand men in new regiments were raised
by private subscription alone. Troubles multiplied
now on all sides ; troubles in India, in Ireland, in
Great Britain, everywhere. France declared war
in 1778, Spain in 1779 ; Holland became an open
enemy in 1780 ; and the Northern Powers formed
an Armed Neutrality to curb our pretensions at sea.
What with regular troops and embodied militia we had
more than one hundred and eighty thousand British
soldiers afoot, besides some twenty thousand Germans ; but this was not enough. Our preparations,
thanks to Parliament's eternal jealousy of the Army,
were made too late. Our military policy was
wrong, for we dispersed our forces so as to endeavour
to hold every point ; and thus we were everywhere
overmatched. The war ended with the loss of
America and very nearly of India also ; of Minorca
in Europe, of Senegal and Goree in West Africa,
and of St Lucia and Tobago in the West Indies.

It might be supposed that England, after such
a disastrous lesson, would have set her military house
in order. Nothing was further from the thoughts of
the Ministry which governed her after the conclusion
of peace. They—Lord North and Mr Fox—were
in such a hurry to get rid of the Army that they discharged every man that they could, and allowed the
garrison of England to sink below seven thousand
men. By this time India demanded a garrison of

over six thousand men, and the Colonies still left
to us, together with Gibraltar, twelve thousand
more. Besides these, the estimates allowed for
thirty-two thousand men in Great Britain and
Ireland ; but not above half of them were forth-
coming because recruits would not enlist ; and the
reason why they did not enlist was because their
pay was insufficient to keep them from starving.
William Pitt the younger took over the administration in 1784, and did admirable service in setting
the national finance upon a sound footing, but would
do nothing for the Army. A dangerous war in
India compelled him to allow some new regiments
to be raised at the expense of the East India Company ; but though thrice in seven years the country
was on the verge of an European war, he did nothing
for the British soldier until 1792 when he grudgingly
doled out to him a small pittance. He suffered the
militia to decay in number and efficiency ; and he
almost destroyed the discipline of the regular troops
by failing to provide them with a military head.
In 1789 the French Revolution broke out, and the
course of events in France was in itself enough to
demand some increase of our military resources ;
but even so late as at the close of 1792 he actually
reduced the British establishment. Within a very
few months he found himself dragged into a war
which to all intents did not end until 1815.

6—2

Pitt's idea was to compel France to submission by taking all her Colonies and ruining all her commerce ; but it was necessary to send troops at short notice to Holland in order to hearten the Dutch to resistance ; and, as there were no others to send, he despatched the Guards. The remainder of the Army, most excellent men but very few in number, he hurried off to the West Indies. This done, he set to work to make the Army, which should have been ready made, according to his father's methods by large bounties and giving commissions to any who would raise companies and regiments. Endless corps of weakly men were thus created, and endless bad officers admitted to the service. The old soldiers in the West Indies did their work admirably, but perished almost to a man, as I shall explain to you in another lecture. In the Low Countries also, where the British were not fairly used by the Allies under whose command they were working, the old soldiers were soon used up ; and we were left without any Army. Even at home, where there was some peril of invasion, Pitt did not pass the nation through the ranks of the Militia, as he should have done, but either enlisted soldiers voluntarily for home service only, or permitted the citizens to enrol themselves in innumerable little useless bodies of Volunteers. The operations in the Low Countries ended disastrously. In the West

Indies practically the whole of the captured islands were recaptured by the French ; and at the close of three years of war Pitt had expended many millions of money, and had nothing to show for it whatever.

By great exertions and appalling sacrifice of life the lost ground in the West Indies was recovered by a rabble of young soldiers, who died like flies as soon as the campaign was over ; and once again we were left without an army. The climax came in 1797 when the Navy mutinied, owing to the small pay and ill-treatment meted out to it ; and it was thought safer, when matters were set right, to raise the pay of the Army also. Now at last there appeared a man who began to set things in order. The Duke of York, second son of King George III, took the post of Commander-in-Chief at the Horse Guards ; reorganised, or rather created, a competent staff at head-quarters, set his face steadily against Pitt's vile methods of raising recruits, and restored the discipline of the Army. In 1799 the declining fortunes of France and the successes of a new coalition against her stimulated Pitt to find some new method of recruiting the Army. He resolved to turn to the Militia as a training ground for the regular troops ; and the Duke of York insisted that the soldiers so raised should be formed into second battalions for existing regiments

instead of being framed into new corps.   Thirty-six
thousand of them were hurried off to Holland without clothing, supplies or transport, and after three
or four barren victories and one serious reverse,
were thankful to return again under a capitulation.
They had been required to do impossibilities and
had failed.   In the following year the same men,
much improved in discipline, were kept idle when
they ought to have been fighting as allies with the
Austrians in Italy ; and thus Napoleon was enabled
to win the victory of Marengo, which made his fortune
as First Consul, and allowed him to trouble Europe
for another fifteen years.   However in 1801 England
at last restored her reputation a little by a brilliant
campaign in Egypt and the capture of the French
army in that country.   To all intents this was our
one solid success in nine years of fighting.   Never
was there more gross mismanagement of a war by
any Minister.

   After a short truce, war broke out again in 1803.
Pitt was not then in power, but was the patron
and more or less the adviser of Addington's weak
administration.   That was the period when Napoleon made great and serious preparations for an
invasion of England ; and it was necessary to take
unprecedented measures for home defence.   Instead
of thinking out some plan for training the entire
manhood of the nation to arms, expanding the

Militia and compelling every man to serve in it,
Addington and his colleagues devised a system
which was one long tissue of absurdities. They
began by instituting a ballot for fifty thousand
Militia, but permitted the ballotted men to provide
substitutes instead of serving in person. The price
of substitutes soon rose to £30, ten times the amount
of the bounty offered to recruits for the Regular
Army ; and as a natural consequence all the men
who should have enlisted in the Army were drawn
into the Militia, while the men who should have
served in the Militia did not serve at all. Having
failed to raise fifty thousand Militia, Ministers
asked for twenty-five thousand more on the same
terms, which raised the price of substitutes still
higher. They then asked for corps of Volunteers
upon very favourable conditions, and then ordained
that fifty thousand more men should be raised by
ballot, once again with substitution permitted, and
should be formed into second battalions to the Regular
Army. They next passed an Act compelling all
able-bodied men to undergo compulsory training,
unless a certain proportion came forward as Volunteers upon less favourable terms than those offered
to the first Volunteers. Thus there were three
different kinds of ballotted men and two different
kinds of Volunteers. The result was that recruiting
for the Regular Army was killed, at great expense,

while the whole of the levies were failures ; and
the only reason was that the Government had not
the courage to insist upon the country's undoubted
right to the service of every able-bodied citizen for
her defence.

Addington was swept out of office ; and Pitt
came in again.   He brought in a bill to form a new
army of Reserve, which was an utter failure ; and he
then fell back on the old expedient of offering a
bounty to Militiamen to enlist in the Regulars.
In this way, which was faithfully followed until
the close of the war in 1814, he raised some semblance
of an Army ; but he did not know how to use it,
and he died in January, 1806, thinking the cause
of Europe hopeless.   A Ministry which included
most of the ablest men in England was formed
upon his death ; and they introduced an Act for
national training to arms, excellent in principle
but not properly worked out in detail, and abolished
the Volunteers.   This was a step in the right direction, but was taken too late.   The Ministry of All
the Talents, as it was called, resigned early in 1807 ;
and then at last the War Office passed into the
hands of a capable man, Lord Castlereagh.   He
began by taking forty thousand men from the
Militia into the Regular Army, and raising as many
—by extremely drastic methods—to refill the empty
ranks of the Militia.   He then devised a scheme

which unfortunately was not enforced, for making
national training a reality ; and finally he established
a new Militia called the Local Militia of two hundred
thousand men for home defence, keeping the old
Militia to furnish recruits for the Regular Army.

Thus for the first time in our history there was
a Regular Army of from forty to fifty thousand men,
fit to go anywhere and do anything, together with
the means of refilling their ranks as fast as they were
depleted by active service.

The number was small but, properly employed,
it could be of great use. In 1807 Napoleon had
shamelessly and treacherously invaded Spain and
Portugal. In 1808 the people of both countries
rose against the invaders, and England's one army
was sent to support them. I told you in my first
lecture that a campaign was like a picnic ; but our
European campaigns of any importance had hitherto been confined to the cockpits, where food was
abundant and wars so frequent that contractors
could always be found to look to the food-supply.
The Peninsula is a very different country, com-
prehending a few fertile districts only together with
a vast deal of barren mountain—a country, according to a well-known saying, where small armies were
beaten and large armies were starved. The French
armies in Spain were large armies, amounting to
three hundred thousand men, and the Spanish

troops, badly led and badly organised, could make no stand against them. How could the British hope with forty thousand men or less to combat three hundred thousand ? In this way. The population of the Peninsula was so bitterly hostile to the invaders that the French could not be said to have any hold of the country, except of such part of it as was actually occupied by their soldiers. It was therefore to the interest of the French, in order to feed their troops as well as to hold down the Spaniards, that their armies should be scattered as much as possible. The very wise and sagacious soldier, Sir Arthur Wellesley, who was charged with the command of our army, reasoned as follows. We have a port of entry and a base of operations at Lisbon, to which we can send by sea everything that we want. Being also masters at sea we can prevent the French from making any use of it ; and they must bring into Spain by land everything that they want. The roads are very bad, so that this in itself will be a heavy task ; and there are so many dangerous defiles to be passed that the Spaniards may always lie in wait to capture French convoys. There is one great advantage for us.

Now as long as we have forty thousand men at Lisbon, the French must always keep rather more in a compact body to watch us, which means that they must collect fifty or sixty thousand men

together instead of leaving them dispersed to hold the
country down ; which means in its turn that so long
as I remain in their front, there must be Spaniards
unsubdued and ready to do mischief to their out-
lying posts and scattered detachments in their rear.
Very well. But what if the French assemble a very
large force, and try to overwhelm me once for all ?
They cannot take a very large force by any one
route, because they live on the country and the
country will not support them ; but if they bring
sixty thousand against my forty thousand, I can
stop them. Twenty-five miles north of Lisbon is
ground that can be made so strong that even Portuguese Militia could hold it, under good leadership,
especially with my army to back them. Moreover
the Portuguese have an ancient law that provides
for the desertion of all villages, the driving off of all
cattle, and the removal of all grain—in fact the
laying waste of their country—before an invader.
If then the French advance against me in Portugal,
I shall retire before them to my fortified lines,
leaving the country a waste behind me. If they
attack me, all the better. I shall beat them. If
they sit down in front of me, I have no objection.
I shall have all the resources of the world behind
me at Lisbon, while they will only have a devastated
wilderness behind them. They may wait for a time,
but they will have to send their troops further and

further afield to scrape together food, and the pea-
sants will cut the throats of all stragglers. Sickness
will increase among their soldiers for want of proper
nourishment ; their numbers will fall lower and
lower and lower ; and at last sheer starvation
will compel them to retreat.

And now, mark how I shall get the better of
them. I shall provide my army with the means of
carrying victuals with it. The task will be extra-
ordinarily difficult, for the country is rough and the
roads so infamous that we cannot use wheeled
vehicles ; but I shall organise a vast train of twelve
to fifteen thousand mules to carry everything that
we want on their backs. The French, a body of
starving men, will have to hurry their retreat, for
they have to pass through a devastated country.
We, with our bellies full, shall be able to follow them
up and cut off thousands of weakly dispirited men.
In time they will reach the fortresses which they
hold on the Spanish frontier, and there we must
stop, while they go back still further to some fertile
district where they will find provisions. But their
army will be absolutely ruined for the time, weakened
by its losses and demoralised by its sufferings. As
I advance I shall establish magazines along the route
so that I may keep my army fed, and threaten their
fortresses. They will be obliged to revictual these
fortresses from time to time, and to do so in presence

of my army they will have to collect once more fifty or sixty thousand men, and leave the country behind them to the mercy of the Spanish guerilla bands. If I can stop them by fighting a general action in a strong position with good hope of success, I shall do so. If I cannot, I shall fall back once more, burning or emptying my magazines, to play the same game again. But the oftener I lead them over the same country, the more it will be exhausted. Their system of living on the country is very wasteful. The brutality of their starving soldiers to the peasantry is driving more and more land out of cultivation ; and the time will come when they will be unable to assemble their troops except at harvest, but will be obliged to keep them dispersed all through the winter in order to keep them alive. It will take them three or four weeks to collect, with enormous difficulty, food and transport enough for even a fortnight's campaign, and I shall use those three or four weeks to make a swift and sudden attack upon their fortresses ; for having the means of feeding my troops, I can do so. They will be obliged to look on helplessly until I have taken the strong places; and, when at last they advance, they will be unable to retake them, until they have driven me back ; and I shall only retire until they have exhausted their provisions, and shall then advance again.

From these fortresses I shall penetrate into Spain
to threaten other fortresses, rousing the whole
country more than ever against the French ; until
at last I compel them to loose their hold upon the
south of Spain, and concentrate a really gigantic
force against me. I shall then retreat as before to
Portugal. They will be unable to keep their
gigantic force for long together from want of food ;
and I shall begin' the whole game all over again ;
while their men waste away by tens of thousands
from fatigue and hardship and incessant petty
attacks of the Spanish guerillas. It is only a question of time before Napoleon is distracted by serious
operations outside Spain ; when once he begins to
reduce his army in the Peninsula, we shall gradually
drive it into France ; and then we shall see how
long Frenchmen will allow it to live on their own
country as it has lived on Spain. I for my part
shall follow it up, paying punctually for everything
that I take, and allowing no plunder ; and we shall
see which army gets on the better.

There in a nutshell is the history of the Peninsular War. Does it not sound simple after the
event ? But think of the sagacity and insight of
the man who perceived all these possibilities before
the event ; and of the courage and force of character
which enabled him to carry his policy into effect.
Patience, the great attribute of Marlborough, was

the quality which shone above all others in Wellington. And remember that he had to subdue not only himself to patience, but his army, and the British nation, and the Spanish nation and the Portuguese nation. Following his difficulties through his correspondence one marvels how ever he overcame them. The British Government, let people say what they will, supported him well in the face of great obstacles and in the teeth of bitter resistance from an unscrupulous Opposition; but they gained greatly from Wellington's moral support. Spain and Portugal had practically no government, and such authority as existed was to a great extent distributed among fools and knaves. In truth Wellington really administered the government of Portugal for four years, besides commanding the British and Portuguese armies in the field. Never allow yourselves to be abridged of your pride in Wellington by petty detractors, British or foreign. German and French writers, for some strange reason, unite to decry him as a commander. Do not listen to them. Not one of them knows anything of any of his campaigns except that of Waterloo. He was a very great commander in every way, and beyond all doubt (at least such is my opinion) the very greatest of his time upon the actual field of battle. He was not a genial character. He had none of Marlborough's irresistible charm, which made even

the privates call him Corporal John.   He was never
loved by man nor woman, nor by any but children
not his own.   By self-imposed discipline—as I
believe—rather than by nature he was cold, hard,
unsympathetic, and inclined to account the individual man as nothing in comparison with the
sanctity of a principle.   Hence he broke the heart
of more than one good officer who had served him
well.   But he was incapable of anything common or
mean ; he was as hard to himself as to the humblest
of his subordinates ; and his conception of duty to
Sovereign and Country was so high, and at the same
time so spontaneous and natural, that his must
always remain the standard by which our public men
will be measured.   No ! if any one ever presumes to
hint to you that Wellington was not a great man,
you may ask him if a small man could constrain
three nations for four years to patience, and raise
the standard of public duty for ever in his own
country.   This is the centenary of his greatest
campaign and most brilliant military achievement ;
but long after they are forgotten men will repeat his
saying " The King's Government must be carried on."

After the twenty-three years of fighting concluded at Waterloo people imagined that wars would
cease.   There was much social and commercial
distress in England ; and as usual the British mind
fastened itself upon the reduction of the Army as

the remedy for all evils. There arose also a political sect which preached the inimitably absurd doctrine that Free Trade would bring about universal peace. The military and naval establishments were cut down to a dangerously low figure ; and all the organisation, which Wellington had created for the feeding of an army, was allowed to decay. At last in 1854 came the war in the Crimea; and there was a repetition of all that had happened in 1792. A small number of very fine regiments was with difficulty scraped together, and sent to the East with no very definite idea as to what they should do, and therefore necessarily without preparation of any kind. Eventually the troops were landed in the Crimea and marched upon Sevastopol. They fought a few magnificent actions, and perished of cold, want and exposure within ten miles of the sea, of which we had absolute command. It was therefore necessary to improvise a new army by the old expedients of bounties, hiring foreign mercenaries, and so forth. Hundreds of boys were sent out to die after the old fashion ; and the Militia were employed, with their own consent, to take over part of the Mediterranean garrisons, and to release the regular troops there for active service. By dint of extravagant expenditure an efficient army was formed within the space of two years, just in time to witness the conclusion of peace.

That was our last European war. It woke us

up a little ; and we were still further roused by the
triumph of the Germans over the French in 1870.
We took our army more or less in hand, improved
the organisation by substituting regiments of two
battalions for regiments of one battalion, and introduced a system of enlisting men not for twenty-one
years with the colours, but for seven with the colours
and five in the Reserve.   The system worked badly
at first, when we had to provide troops for small
colonial expeditions ; but the faults were gradually
amended ;   and the organisation stood the test
fairly well in 1899 and 1900 in South Africa.   We
can now send 150,000 men abroad perfectly equipped,
which is more than we could ever do before; but
other nations count their armies by millions, and in
reality we are as far behindhand as ever we were.
We have no means of replacing those 150,000 within
six months, which would be necessary in case of a
great war ; much less have we means of expanding
their numbers to twice 150,000 and keeping their
ranks filled ; and we have no efficient force of any
strength, not even the old Militia, for home defence,
while our 150,000 are abroad.   Do not think that I
am "talking politics."   I am only stating plain facts.
I cannot discuss, nor even propound, the questions
which these facts suggest ; but I cannot avoid the
assertion of the facts themselves, for they are
essential to our understanding of our subject—
they are indeed the pith of British military history.

LECTURE III

BRITISH COLONIAL CAMPAIGNS

I PROPOSE in my present lecture to deal with our
colonial campaigns at large.   You will recognise at
once that a colonial campaign differs from other campaigns in one essential point.   One does not attempt
to form colonies in any but an empty or comparatively empty country, first because in any other
there is no room for colonists, and secondly because
a numerous native population may be subdued but
cannot be displaced.   It is therefore imperative that
the indigenous inhabitants of a country, whither
settlers propose to emigrate, shall be few ; and it is
practically as imperative that, unless their numbers
are so scanty as to be negligible, they shall be of
inferior civilisation, so that they may not be able to
fight the settlers on equal terms.   Now what do
inferiority of civilisation and paucity of numbers
mean, militarily speaking, to the civilised invader ?
They mean, first of all, no roads or at the very best
rough tracks, and no bridges over rivers ; they mean
further rude cultivation and very small stores, if any,
of cereal food.   This signifies in its turn that the
great problem of the campaign will be how to feed your
force in the field, or as we now call it the problem of
transport (for the campaign will be more than ever a

picnic) and of supply. In the matter of actual combat the uncivilised enemy will have the advantage
certainly of perfect adaptation to the climate,
intimate knowledge of the country, and generally
of stronger physical endurance, greater rapidity of
movement, and decided superiority in eyesight and
hearing. His disadvantages will be inferior organisation, inferior armament, and inexperience of the need
for providing a great multitude with food at a
distance from its provision-grounds. Speaking
generally the sound principle of savage warfare is
this—to equip yourself with a good service for
transport and supply, march up to your enemy, sit
down and fortify yourself in a strong position.
Your enemy must then do one of three things :
attack you, in which case he is sure to be defeated ;
move on ; or starve. He is not likely to attempt
attack after a lesson or two, and therefore as a rule
he will move on. You then move after him and sit
down again, destroying or appropriating his provision-grounds and capturing his cattle, as you find
opportunity. By this method you must infallibly
bring him to submission. It was thus that George
Monk subdued the Highlands.

It is not, however, by any means always possible
to pursue this policy. Your adversaries may be
dwellers in forests, such as the Red Indian ; or in
wooded mountains, such as the Kaffir and the Carib ;

or defended in part by an arid wilderness, as are the Soudanis. Moreover they may be a people of military instincts and organisation, with their own skilful system of tactics, and a sense of honour which prefers death to disgrace. Such were that most gallant race, the Zulus. Or they may be of a magnificent strength and stature with a fanatical contempt for death, as the Dervishes. Or they may combine something of the Zulu with their own very elaborate system of fortification, as the Maoris. Each race and country presents its own peculiar features and problems, which need to be considered and solved upon their merits. But speaking generally the difference between the civilised and uncivilised fighter is this, that the one takes care to carry his food with him, whereas the other does not.

Now what is true of a savage country at the outset usually remains true for some time, indeed for a very long time, after civilised settlement has begun. The supplies of food are small, for a small population cannot grow much produce, and has no occasion to lay in a great store ; roads and means of communication are few and bad ; and there is hardly a bridge to be found. If all the miles of macadamised road existent in the whole of the British Empire at this moment were added together, I doubt if they would equal, or even nearly equal, those of the British Isles alone. Bearing these things in mind, and remembering that two centuries ago there were very few paved roads in Europe, and not a single macadamised road until less than a century ago, let us look for a time at our colonial Military History.

Our earliest settlements were made in North America and the West Indies; the latter slightly earlier than the former but to all intent contemporaneously; and the Dutch and French were there very nearly as early as we ourselves, at the beginning of the seventeenth century. In North America the settlers naturally established themselves first on the coast, using the great rivers as water-ways to penetrate into the back country. The Dutch in the first instance chose one of the most important of those rivers, building the town of New Amsterdam at the mouth of the Hudson. The French took perhaps the most important of all, the St Lawrence, founding Quebec near its mouth and Montreal a little higher up. Lastly the Spaniards held the south and the mouth of the Mississippi, so far away that they were of small concern either to the French or the English. South of the St Lawrence the English colonists scattered themselves in the course of the seventeenth century along more than a thousand miles of coast from the Kennebec to the Savannah. Quebec itself was captured in 1627 from the French but, in spite of the protests of far-seeing men, was given back under a treaty of peace in 1632. New

Amsterdam was taken from the Dutch in 1664, and retained as New York. In their early days most of these settlements came into hostile collision with the Indians at one time or another, but were able to hold their own, for they had brought with them over the ocean the old English principle that all able-bodied men were liable to service for domestic defence. New York, however, did even better; for that Colony specially cultivated the friendship of the Five Nations—the most formidable of the Indians—for the sake not only of the fur-trade, but of protection against other Indians and dangerous neighbours on the north.

Those dangerous neighbours were of course the French. Their colonies on the St Lawrence were strictly military, the settlers being mostly old soldiers who received their grants of land in reward for past and in consideration of future service; while the government was despotic and centred in a military officer of experience and ability. The younger French settlers were always attracted by the free life of the Indians in the forest; hence every man was a skilful woodman, a good marksman and a trained canoe-man, in fact a better sportsman and warrior than colonist. Moreover they and the Jesuits, who both ministered to their spiritual needs and laboured to convert and rule the Indians, were enterprising and intrepid explorers. They soon

wandered through the whole chain of lakes, found
the rivers Illinois and Wisconsin running out of
Lake Michigan, and followed them down the whole
course of the Mississippi to New Orleans, taking
possession of the entire country in the name of
Louis XIV. This they accomplished in 1680, five
years before the death of King Charles II ; and we
ought always to salute the gallant French nation in
honour of the brave men who essayed and accomplished this great feat of exploration. From that
moment the French conceived the notion of getting
behind us along the entire length of the continent,
and confining us to the coast, with the power always
of coming down upon our settlements from the rear
at any convenient opportunity, and driving us into
the sea. It is a very general system with the French,
which they have attempted in our own time in West
Africa. They always explore and they always make
maps, being a practical people, and the result is that
they always get the better of us in disputes over
boundaries. Their strong points in America in the
seventeenth century were their unity and enterprise.
Their weak points were their numbers (for they did
not exceed twelve thousand) and the fact that they
raised no great quantity of food.

The English settlers on the other hand were
agriculturalists, and each community was distinct,
jealous and self-centred. In New York there was

a large trade with the Indians ; and the pious
Quakers of Pennsylvania and Rhode Island used to
finance pirates who at one time nearly swept our
East Indian trade off the seas. But for the most
part they quietly tilled the soil, or in the north went
fishing ; nor could any power induce even a few of
them to unite their forces against the French.   They
would invade each other, for they were a most
cantankerous people, but would never make a
combined effort against the common enemy.   New
York and New England, being nearest to the French,
made endeavours from time to time to drive them
out, but always failed owing to provincial jealousies,
want of discipline, want of organisation, want of
efficient leaders.   There are two waterways, broken
in places by rapids, which, as you know, lead from
New York to the St Lawrence ; the one by the
Mohawk and Lake Ontario, the other by the Hudson
and Lakes George and Champlain ; and these waterways were the scene of all the fighting for the mastery
of Canada.   In 1690 and 1691 New York and New
England made a desperate but inefficient attempt to
take Quebec.   They failed miserably, though New
England alone could pit ninety thousand settlers
against the French twelve thousand.   The French,
united and well commanded, took the offensive,
broke down the power of the Five Indian Nations
—the principal defensive barrier of the English

settlements—and the Colonies were reduced to
shrieking to England for help.

Queen Anne sent an expedition to the St
Lawrence in 1711, which failed owing to the in-
competence of the commander; but none the less
at the Peace of Utrecht France ceded to us Nova
Scotia. Thereupon the French proceeded to fortify
all the commanding points on the lakes (remember
that the waterways were the only ways by which
an army could be supplied), and established a naval
station on Cape Breton to harass British shipping
in future wars. This was the celebrated fortress
of Louisburg; and the building of it was a very
costly mistake. Why ? Because it was situated in
a barren territory which could raise nothing and
support nothing, wherefore Louisburg could only
be provisioned from without and from the sea.
Without superiority at sea therefore Louisburg must
starve ; with superiority at sea it was a superfluity.
The rival settlers and their Indians continued to
raid each other perpetually along their frontiers
until the War of the Austrian Succession brought
about overt hostilities ; and then in 1745 the forces
of New England, commanded by a lawyer and with
the help of a British squadron, besieged and took
Louisburg. This was a brilliant feat for amateurs,
though of course the most difficult part of the work
was done by British sailors ; but upon the peace of

1748 the British Government very wisely restored Louisburg, preferring to keep Madras in the East Indies in its place. On the other hand the British established a military settlement of old soldiers at Halifax.

The French now began seriously to pursue their policy of establishing themselves in rear of the British colonies, by forcibly occupying two British settlements on the Ohio, and building a chain of forts to maintain the communications between these, Lake Erie and Montreal. The Governor of Virginia sent a young officer of Militia, named George Washington, to tell them to go, but was answered that the French had no intention of moving. The Colonies with the greatest difficulty were brought to vote a small sum of money for a force to drive the French out; and Washington advanced again to Ohio, only to be surrounded by superior numbers and forced to surrender. This might, one would have thought, have roused the Colonies; but with the exception of New England, which was burning to capture Canada, one and all showed the completest apathy. The Americans had, and still have, all the modern English indifference to national duty and military preparations. To the enduring shame of the Colonies, therefore, application was made to England for help; and two regiments were sent out under General Braddock, a capable but narrow-minded officer, who had no idea of military operations except as carried out in a European cock-pit. His difficulties were great, for his march lay for one hundred miles through dense forests, which provided neither forage for animals nor food for men ; and, when animals have to carry their own food, they have little strength to carry more. The only chance was to move lightly and rapidly ; whereas on the contrary Braddock encumbered himself with waggons which necessitated an advanced party of three hundred axe-men to clear away trees and obstacles. Nor did he make any effort to train his troops to bush-fighting ; and hence when caught at a disadvantage by the enemy on the march, they were seized with panic and cut to pieces. An advance of the local forces of New England towards the St Lawrence was also a failure, owing to the usual indiscipline of the Colonial levies, and the entire campaign ended in disaster.

A few more troops were sent from England in the following year, 1756, together with a new general ; but he could accomplish little, having inadequate forces and being unable to persuade the Colonists to provide more. The conduct of campaigns by New England lawyers was in fact most wasteful and inefficient. In 1757, as we have seen, Pitt came to the head of affairs ; but he had not time to make provision for a more effective management of the

war in America ; and all the successes of the year
were on the side of the French. At last in 1758 a
new commander-in-chief, General Jeffery Amherst,
was appointed ; the regular soldiers were increased
to the number of twenty-six thousand ; and Pitt
undertook to clothe, equip, feed and arm twenty-five
thousand Colonial troops, leaving to the Colonies only
the expense of paying them. Louisburg was besieged and taken by Amherst, and the French were
driven from the Ohio ; but an advance of sixteen
thousand men towards the St Lawrence was checked
by a disgraceful reverse, owing to the incapacity of
the British commander. Amherst took personal
command on this side in the following year, leaving
Wolfe to attack Quebec ; and in 1760 the resistance
of the French entirely collapsed. It needed only
careful organisation and endless pains in the troublesome work of bringing forward food for the troops
to render success certain ; and yet the Americans
could not do it. Beyond all question there were
brains in America fully equal to the business of
divining exactly what would be wanted ; indeed
Benjamin Franklin had to do with the organisation
of Braddock's expedition ; but there were no disciplined men who could be trusted to do exactly what
they were told. The British soldiers were no doubt,
to the Colonial mind, helpless and unhandy beyond
expression ; but they knew how to obey. If told

to do a thing to-day at ten o'clock, they did not wait till to-morrow at three—which is the Colonial way—and it is only by punctuality that a campaign can be even begun. Selfishness, jealousy and indiscipline were the causes why the Americans, notwithstanding their huge superiority in number of population, were unable to conquer the French in Canada without a British army to help them. Had the position of the two nations been reversed, the French would have driven us from Canada in twelve months.

The result of our exertions in behalf of the Colonies is well known. Having delivered them from a dangerous neighbour, we asked them to share with us the burden of Imperial defence. They admitted the justice of the claim, but declined to satisfy it. When we endeavoured to solve the problem by means of the Imperial Parliament, they resented it with furious violence. English politicians, too many of them from factious spite, but a few from higher motives, supported and encouraged them. The question of Imperial defence was lost sight of. There was mismanagement on our side, gross provocation on the side of the Colonists; and the quarrel finally issued in war. The Americans took the offensive and made a dash upon Canada, whence they were with some difficulty repulsed. We recaptured New York; and then, by extraordinary blundering at home, General Burgoyne was ordered

to advance south from Canada upon the supposition
that General Howe would advance northward to
meet him from New York; instead of which Howe
sailed to the Delaware and captured Philadelphia.
Burgoyne meanwhile endeavoured to do as he was
bidden; but from want of land-transport found that
continued progress through the forest was impossible.
His only chance was, if he could, to capture one of
the enemy's magazines by surprise; and it was the
miscarriage of an attempt to do this which first
entangled him in serious danger. He plunged deeper
and deeper into a circle of enemies, and was surrounded and compelled to surrender; but his
campaign was in reality wrecked by the difficulty of
transport and supply in a wild country. In one
space of twenty miles, for instance, he was obliged
to fell trees and build forty bridges over rivers and
creeks, with the result that he took precisely twenty
days to traverse the distance. Invasion on such
terms, when the whole population of a country is
hostile, is almost impossible of success. Yet
strangely enough the whole object of the movement
from north and south along the line of the Hudson
was to secure the line of the river, and cut off the
colonies to the east from the colonies on the west of
it. For the cereal supplies of the American army
were on the west bank, and the meat supplies on the
east; and to deprive them of either would force them

to fight or to disband themselves. Thus, you see,
the question of subsistence was at the root of the
whole matter.

The disaster at Saratoga brought the French as
allies to the Americans; and it was the supremacy
of the French fleet on the coast at a critical moment
which decided the issue of the war. There was
fighting, and hard fighting, in the southern colonies;
but the Americans would never have beaten us
without the help of the French. Had they been
really in earnest they could have driven us from the
country in twelve months, but they were not in
earnest. They wanted other people to do their
fighting for them, whether they were contending
against France in 1757 or England in 1780; and
by great good fortune they found such other people
ready to their hand. A few noble and patriotic men
did indeed their utmost duty to their country; but
they were very few. The rest were unwilling to
make the sacrifice demanded of them by service in
the field and submission to discipline. Hence their
Government was driven to cruelty and double-
dealing of every kind to force their British prisoners
to enter the American ranks, so as to save selfish
citizens from risking their worthless skins. In fact
when one compares the resistance of the three
million Americans in 1776–1781 with that of the
few hundred thousand Boers in 1899–1902, it is

impossible to regard the American rebellion with
any great respect.

In 1812 we were again embroiled with America
chiefly owing to the intrigues of Napoleon, but in
great measure also through the hostility of two of
the Presidents. As usual, these two officials and
their supporters counted upon Napoleon to fight
their battles for them, and made no preparations
for war, thinking that they would be able to take
Canada with ease from us, who had the great
Emperor and all his forces upon our hands. They
were egregiously undeceived. Their naval officers and
sailors acquitted themselves admirably, though their
ships were too few to make head against us in the
open sea. Their troops were for long beneath contempt, owing to want of training and discipline. We
had so much upon our hands that we could spare
few soldiers to meet them; but the Americans never
succeeded, in spite of greatly superior numbers,
in taking Canada; and at last they were glad to
make peace without gaining any of the objects
for which they had fought, being absolutely exhausted and ruined by our naval blockade. But it
is to be noticed that, as usual, transport and supply
were the great difficulties on both sides and that,
setting aside some raids on our part which were not
always successful, the main fighting took place on
the waterway of the great lakes, simply because that

was the only quarter in which either side could feed even a small army. In fact it was impossible, for want of decent roads, to bring forward supplies except by water ; and success or failure to either party depended wholly upon naval supremacy on the lakes. When we held it we beat the Americans, when the Americans held it they beat us ; so that practically this was a naval war albeit fought inland.

Let us pass next to the West Indies. Where islands are concerned, of course naval superiority is essential to every successful campaign, otherwise you cannot bring either troops or stores to the scene of action. The Antilles are for the most part of volcanic formation, mountainous, if a height of three to four thousand feet may be said to make a mountain, rugged, and in the majority of cases covered with forest, cultivation generally being confined to the lower hills and valleys. Situated between the 10th and 23rd degrees of North latitude, they lie well within the Tropic of Cancer ; and the climate is consequently such that white men cannot breed and thrive there. Roads in the great majority of the islands are few, and such as there are frequently traverse ground so steep that they are paved and not macadamised, lest the surface should be washed away by the heavy tropical rains. By far the greater number of such roads (I except the island of Barbados) are mere tracks, narrow, rough and unfit for vehicles. Bridges are even fewer than roads, though the islands with which we are chiefly concerned are furrowed by torrents, which have cut deep ravines and valleys in their rush from the mountains down to the sea. Hence what with forests, streams, hills and valleys as steep as those of the Highlands, it is not easy to move about most of the islands. All labour was formerly done by negro slaves imported from West Africa, whose descendants—now for three generations free—still form the mass of the population. These negroes to a certain extent cultivate provision-grounds for themselves ; but the islands are none of them self-supporting in the matter of food ; and for full two centuries they have been supplied with flour, maize, salt fish and salt pork from America. Strategically they fall into two groups : the Windward, comprising the chain of islets which runs for some six hundred miles north and westward from Trinidad to St Thomas ; and the Leeward, consisting of the far larger islands of Porto Rico, St Domingo, Jamaica and Cuba, which run nearly due west from St Thomas. Everything in the West Indies is windward or leeward, that is to say is considered in respect of its situation towards the south-easterly trade-wind, which in the days of sailing ships was a very important matter. Say, for instance, that the General in Jamaica asked for reinforcements from the General at Barbados, the most leewardly from the most windwardly of our possessions ; the General in Barbados had to think twice before sending them because, though they would probably reach Jamaica in a week, they could not be sure of beating back in three months. In fact no captain in old days would have attempted such a thing, for it would have been quite as speedy and far less exhausting to sail back to England by a circuitous course and make a fresh start for Barbados from thence. So too between any two islands the same question of windward and leeward was equally cogent. Martinique, the French head-quarters in the Windward group, is little over one hundred miles from Barbados, the English head-quarters ; but while you may sail from Barbados to Martinique in twelve hours, you will not beat back in less than three or four days.

The Spaniards, as you know, were the first in the West Indies, but they troubled themselves little about the Windward islets, occupying by preference the great islands of Porto Rico, St Domingo, Cuba and Jamaica. We and the French, however, began at much the same time to occupy the islets to windward, which are all of about the size of the Isle of Wight, and we did a good deal of petty squabbling over them. These little places very soon became enormously rich. Sugar, indigo and spices, produced by servile labour, brought in enormous profits ;

while incidentally the contract for providing the
Spanish islands with slaves—known as the Assiento—
which we held for a great many years, was highly
lucrative. Even in the reign of Charles II a Jamaican
planter with an income of £12,000 a year—worth
say £50,000 in these days—was not considered extra-
ordinarily wealthy; and for nearly two centuries the
West Indian was the most powerful mercantile
interest in the British islands.

With aboriginal inhabitants, or Caribs, we never
had any very serious trouble, for they were few in
the islands which we occupied; and in fact though,
when incited by our European enemies, they gave
occasional annoyance, they were never the subject
of any serious military expedition until 1772, when
a hybrid race, bred of yellow Carib and African
negro, both brave and vigorous, became rebellious
in St Vincent. There were only fifteen hundred
of them, men, women, and children; but it took
three thousand soldiers and marines, backed by two
or three ships of war, five entire months to force
them to submission, so formidable were the difficulties of feeding the troops in the thick forest and
deep ravines of the interior. Few horses and mules
were bred in the Windward islands, so that all the
supplies were carried on the heads of negroes. Had
the Caribs, therefore, been a really formidable fighting race, it would have taken us long to conquer

the West Indies. As things were, we imported the
negroes, who bred fast and soon outnumbered the
aborigines ; and thus we either compelled the Caribs
to move, or agreed to let them have some patch of
territory for their own. Of course the slaves were
not quite an element of safety, and the whole of the
West Indies lived in constant dread of a servile war.
Hence a little garrison was generally kept by every
nation in every island ; and at least one fort was
erected, as a rule, for defence of the capital and its
harbour against both foreign and domestic enemies,
while smaller works covered less important towns.

An expedition to the West Indies therefore meant
almost certainly something in the nature of a siege
until the fort and town were captured ; and, when
that was accomplished, the conquest, so far as white
men were concerned, was complete. For in a small
island it was inevitable that the capital should be
situated by the best harbour ; and, when this harbour was in an invader's hands, he could land as
many troops as he wished with ease, while he was
also master of all supplies of food, which naturally
were stored in the town. The operations, however,
though short were sure to be arduous owing to the
heat of the climate and the ruggedness of the ground ;
and therefore it was important that they should be
undertaken in the cool season, that is to say between
November and May, in which latter month the heat

and the rains begin to increase and the climate becomes, or at any rate became, unhealthy. The confinement of operations to this season is the more imperative, since between May and October there is always the danger of hurricanes, and the harbours in which a ship can lie with safety during a hurricane in the West Indies are not many. You must remember that a hurricane is not a mere storm—it is a devouring devastation before which no tree and none but the stoutest houses, carefully equipped for resistance, can hope to stand.

Our first serious state-directed expedition to the West Indies was that despatched by Cromwell to St Domingo in 1654. We were not at war with Spain at the time, and the enterprise was simply a piece of piracy; but it was equipped on a great scale, the fleet numbering sixty-five sail and the troops six thousand men. It was intended that the West Indian and American colonies should furnish contingents of soldiers; and, when St Domingo had been taken, to use it as a base of attack against all the Spanish possessions in the South Atlantic. The expedition, from want of experience, was ill-equipped; the men, hastily raised levies, were of poor quality; and the armament did not sail until the end of December, two months too late. The descent upon St Domingo was a disgraceful and disastrous failure; fleet and army quarrelled violently; and the only

result of the enterprise was the bloodless capture
of Jamaica, after which fleet and army returned
home, leaving a garrison behind them.   Yellow fever
broke out immediately and the garrison was almost
annihilated.   In October, 1655, reinforcements arrived, and began at once to die at the rate of twenty
men a day.   Fresh reinforcements followed in 1656,
and in a few months two-thirds of these were dead.
At last the sickness abated.   An attempt of the
Spaniards to recapture the island in 1658 was beaten
off, and Jamaica has remained under the English
flag ever since.

Here was a warning for all time as to the conduct
of expeditions to the West Indies.   Care must be
taken for good understanding between army and
navy ; and the fleet must sail from England at latest
in October.   We shall see how far this warning has
been observed.   The next important expedition to
the West Indies was sent by King William in 1695
to root out the French who had established themselves at the western end of St Domingo, now called
Haiti, and who were threatening Jamaica from
thence.   This armament did not sail till January,
three months too late, and consequently did not
begin operations till May.   In four months over a
thousand out of the thirteen hundred soldiers had
died ; while the quarrels between the naval and military commanders banished all hope of solid success.

The next great tropical expedition undertaken was that of 1740–1 against Carthagena on the Spanish main, but little outside the beat of our West Indian squadrons. The enterprise was prompted by sheer greed of gain ; the troops were young and raw recruits (for of course we had no old soldiers) and numbered six thousand ; American levies to the number of four thousand were sent from Jamaica to join them ; the whole were shamefully ill-equipped ; and finally the armament sailed four months too late. It was exactly the story of St Domingo over again. The military commander died on the voyage, and his successor, a feeble creature, was treated with the greatest contempt by the naval officers. However, the force reached Carthagena, and the troops were landed ; but the General, mistrusting himself and his men, was so slow and dilatory in his movements that he delayed the decisive attack until late in April, and was then repulsed. Sickness, lead and steel had already reduced his force from nine thousand to little over six thousand effectives, and on the night of the defeat the yellow fever fell upon the unhappy army in earnest. In three days—think of this appalling visitation—in three days the effective men had sunk from sixty-six hundred to thirty-two hundred ; and in ten days more only a thousand were fit to be landed against an enemy. Reduced to a mere shadow, the

expedition returned to Jamaica, but the yellow fever
went with it ; and, within twelve months of the
arrival of the original armament in the tropics, its
numbers had shrunk from nine thousand to fewer
than three hundred fit for duty. At the beginning
of 1742 these were joined by a reinforcement of
three thousand men. Within a month a thousand
of these were sick or dead. A thousand more died
before October, and at last the force practically
disappeared. Of the four thousand Americans only
three hundred lived to return home ; of the nine
thousand British a bare one in ten survived. This
on the whole is the most terrible story that I know
in British military history ; but perhaps I am led
to think so by Smollett's vivid picture of its horrors
in *Roderick Random*. I remember that I read that
book for the first time when I was an undergraduate
at Trinity, little thinking that I should live to proclaim the fact to a Trinity audience. Every one of
you ought to read it if you have not already done so,
to learn at first hand what was meant by naval and
military service in the eighteenth century.

Here was another warning to strengthen the first.
But meanwhile the West Indies grew and grew in
wealth, and were more and more coveted by all nations.
Hence the great William Pitt himself was eager to
appropriate as many islands as possible, setting thus
a very evil example to his son. At the end of 1758

six battalions were sent out to capture Guadeloupe,
which they duly did, being handled with great skill
by General Barrington, before the hurricane season
began. Three of the six battalions were left there as
a garrison, and, before the year was out, about half
of them had died. In 1762 Pitt's successor, acting
upon his designs, sent eight thousand men to capture
the remaining French islands; and, this being accomplished, not without heavy loss from sickness,
the remnant of the force joined a detachment of
troops under Lord Albemarle in the siege of Havana.
Twelve thousand men were employed in this siege,
which lasted two months, and was one of the most
deadly in which British soldiers were ever engaged.
Before its close one brigade of four battalions was
reduced to twenty men fit for duty. Over five
thousand men were buried in Cuba alone in four
months, while hundreds more perished both there
and in North America, whither they had been transported in the hope of saving their lives.

Several French islands passed into our possession
at the Peace of Paris, all of course demanding garrisons which required to be totally renewed every two
years; but Guadeloupe, Martinique and St Lucia
were left to the French; and it was in order to gain
a safe harbour in St Lucia, commanding the French
naval base at Martinique close by, that a descent
was made upon it in 1778 by five thousand British

troops from America. The operations were conducted in a masterly fashion both by sea and land ; and the capture of the island atoned in some measure for that of sundry British islands by the French. But the virulence of yellow fever was everywhere terrible ; and the usual mortality was heightened in 1780 by a hurricane of peculiar violence. In Barbados four thousand human beings, nine thousand cattle and horses, and smaller stock without number were destroyed in a few hours. Still, by laying the forest flat and thus destroying the harbour for mosquitoes, the hurricane abated the sickness in St Lucia.

And now we come to the war of the French Revolution, when Pitt thought to compel France to submission by taking all her colonies and depriving her of all colonial produce, whether as a luxury or as a source of revenue. France had but three islands to windward, Martinique, Guadeloupe and St Lucia and to leeward the western end of St Domingo, called Haiti ; but all were flourishing settlements ; and Haiti was considered the richest possession in the world, its produce being valued at four millions annually. All three had been shaken, and Haiti half-ruined, by the doctrines of the National Assembly, which had not only abolished slavery, but preached the doctrine of equality among all men to such effect that the negroes had risen and either massacred or driven out two-thirds of the whites. In the hope of restoring order and regaining their wealth the remainder of the whites invited the General at Jamaica to occupy their territory, an offer at which that officer grasped eagerly, knowing by reputation the wealth of the place. Shortly afterwards at the end of 1793, but two months too late, Pitt sent seven thousand troops under General Grey and a fleet under Sir John Jervis, better known as Lord St Vincent, to capture the French Windward islands. The two commanders were excellent men in their professions, and on affectionate terms with each other. Their operations prospered. The three islands were taken after two months hard work ; and then with the coming of the unhealthy season the men began to die. Emissaries, one of them a West Indian mulatto of great energy and ability, arrived from France with arms and reinforcements, proclaimed the equality of all men, and stirred up the negroes to root the English out. The negroes responded ; and not in the French islands only, but in all that had ever been French, they rose in insurrection against the whites. Meanwhile Pitt had sent the British regiments no reinforcements, no stores, no clothing ; and they had now a most formidable task before them. It was no longer a case of meeting white men of like weakness and disabilities with themselves, but of contending with

black men to whom the climate was favourable and
who knew every inch of the country.

By the end of the year 1794 five out of seven
thousand of Grey's men had died, and Guadeloupe
had been recaptured by the French. By the summer
of 1795 St Lucia had also been recaptured ; and
the British even in their own islands of St Vincent
and Grenada had been dispossessed of all but
the two forts and capitals. Scattered regiments of
boys sent out by Pitt sufficed only to fill the graveyards, for they could not stand the active work
of the campaign ; and at last Pitt was obliged to
despatch a fresh army of seventeen thousand men
to recover the lost ground. The expedition, owing
to the usual blundering, started too late, and the
troops were of the worst quality, young, untrained
and of poor physique. However, thanks to their
commander, Sir Ralph Abercromby, they managed
to recapture the lost islands, which by that time had
been reduced to desolation by the insurgent negroes ;
and then of course they died like flies. Meanwhile
ever since 1793 Haiti had swallowed up more and
more troops, the black insurgents opposing the
British most gallantly but proving far less deadly
than the yellow fever. Year after year reinforcements arrived to complete the work of conquest,
and year after year the army was reduced to a shadow
before it could accomplish its task. But Pitt, still

insatiable, sent Abercromby out a second time in 1797 to capture Trinidad and Porto Rico, which latter island by great good fortune was too strong for him. It was not until 1798 that the bickering over these miserable islands ceased, and even then by no fault of Pitt's. It was a military officer who decided on his own responsibility to evacuate Haiti, against the wishes of the Government, but none too soon. By that time Pitt's military policy, so called, had cost us 100,000 men, but had not contributed in the slightest degree to check the aggression of Revolutionary France.

After this awful lesson the Government began to train black soldiers to take the place of white in future West Indian expeditions ; while the white garrisons were largely composed of foreigners and battalions of convicts. But while struggling to create an army at home by the mistaken methods which I have already described to you, Addington opened the second part of the war by capturing St Lucia, Tobago and Dutch Guiana, thus multiplying unhealthy stations which ate steadily into our own strength without diminishing that of the enemy. Ultimately a series of expeditions, exceedingly well managed, swept the whole of the West Indies, excepting the Spanish, into our net, and put an end to all warfare in that quarter for the remainder of the war. By the peace of 1814 Martinique and

Guadeloupe were restored to France, but were
recaptured by us in 1815 during the Hundred Days,
and then finally given back to be captured no more.
The sequel is melancholy enough. For about a
quarter of a century after Waterloo our miserable
pittance of an army was hidden away in great
measure in the Islands; and then suddenly the
British nation in one of those fits of conscientiousness
to which it is occasionally subject, decided practically to destroy these possessions by abolishing
slavery and repealing the duties which protected
their produce. The abolition of slavery was no
doubt a good thing, but as it extended at first to the
English islands only, its immediate effect was to
give a tremendous impulse to the slave trade, with
all its horrors, in the French, Dutch and Spanish
islands. To all intent it penalised our own islands
to the advantage of the Spanish islands, and favoured
our few negroes to the prejudice of ten times their
number of others. This evil after some years passed
away, as the abolition of slavery was accepted by
other countries; but the West Indies have never
recovered from the shock of the double blow. Moreover, apart from these two legislative enactments,
Pitt's policy of ruining France by taking her colonies
has resulted in the ruin of the colonies for the benefit
of France. For, being deprived of all colonial produce, French men of science sought out the means

of growing some of that produce in France itself; and hence arose the manufacture of sugar from the root of the beet, and an immense industry not in France only but all over Europe, which drives the best West Indian sugar out of the market. So little can even great men foresee the consequences of their actions.

Thus the West Indies have fallen for ever from their high estate; and it is only by an actual visit to them that we can divine what they once were. Ruined forts, ruined barracks, ruined store-houses, old guns slowly mouldering away, pyramids of round shot so welded together by rust that they cannot be moved—these are the more visible tokens of past greatness. But a searching enquirer will turn his steps to the desolate graveyards, and tearing his way through rank herbage and tropical scrub will approach the crumbling head-stones, and there he may read—or at least I could read thirty years ago— what a visitation of yellow fever meant in the old days. Field-officers, captains, lieutenants, ensigns, sergeants, corporals, drummers, rank and file of battalion after battalion lie there in row upon row, as if on parade, while the land-crabs hurry from grave to grave, and deadly snakes lie coiled upon the heaps of crumbling stones which once were monuments. I know no more melancholy sight than this. How many British soldiers and sailors lie in

these and other unknown graves in the Caribbean
Islands ?   I know not ; but the lowest figure that
I should suggest would be three hundred thousand,
and the highest perhaps half a million.   And the
pity of it is that the value of the islands disappeared
just when the means of economising life began to
be perfected.   The formation of negro regiments,
though bitterly opposed by the planters, who
dreaded the slightest emergence of the black race
from the status of servitude, was a great and
courageous act of statesmanship—courageous because formerly the West Indian interest could muster
a solid phalanx of eighty votes in the House of
Commons, and was thus able to overset a Government.   Now too in these later days yellow fever
has yielded up its secrets to science, and can be
disarmed of its terrors.   But it is too late.   No one
cares for the West Indies nowadays.   No one re-
members that at one time Cuba was deemed more
valuable than Madras.   The whole of the Antilles
are now entrusted to the protection of one white
battalion, one black battalion, and two companies
of artillery ; and the great bulk of these men are kept
there not for the sake of the once wealthy sugar
islands, but to ensure the safety of the naval station
of Bermuda.   One could contemplate such a change
with equanimity but for the recollection of perhaps
half a million lives sacrificed to no purpose.

I turn now to the seat of the most difficult of all of our colonial wars, South Africa ; the most difficult because it is of vast extent, inhabited by warlike natives for the most part, and without waterways. Our first attack upon it in 1795, when we were opposed by Dutch troops and Boers only, is remarkable as an example of a campaign conducted by three thousand white soldiers without any transport whatever, and without even gun-teams. The distance from the base, Simonstown, to the objective, Capetown, was only twelve miles, nearly all through deep sand ; but the enemy were as strong as the invaders ; and, when everything has to be dragged by white men's arms or carried upon white men's backs, the difficulties of movement are so great—especially if the march be opposed at every step—as to be almost insuperable. However, a large proportion of the force was turned into beasts of burden, and their numbers were supplemented by blue-jackets and marines ; the general having wisely decided that both Services should share alike in the drudgery of transport and in the more congenial work of fighting. Thus Capetown, by a tremendous effort, was taken for the first time. When we attacked it again in 1806 we disembarked at a different point ; and the enemy's general was obliging enough to come out to meet us at once, and to be beaten. Thus our force, about six thousand strong,

was enabled to victual itself from the fleet at the
end of the first day's advance, and to march into
Capetown at the end of the second.

Since then we have fought many wars in South
Africa against both natives and Dutch colonists ;
and in all of them the main difficulty has been that
of feeding the troops. There is of course the
country-transport which is familiar to us—the huge
tilted waggons with their eight yoke of oxen, each in
the charge of two skilled natives—of which we heard
so much twelve years ago. Of its kind it is good.
But such large vehicles and teams are very unwieldy ;
they must be left in charge of natives who cannot be
trusted (and small blame to them) not to run away
in moments of danger ; and lastly the ox, though
patient, plucky and persevering to an uncommon
degree, has his defects as a draft animal. He is very
slow and he must not be hurried ; he needs time to
chew the cud after feeding ; and he cannot work
with the full power of the sun beating upon his back.
In fact he has his times and seasons which must be
carefully observed, or he will die ; and he is sensitive
not only to sun, but also to cold and wet. The enemy,
being fully aware of his limitations, can foresee their
effect upon the movements of the force opposed to
them, and can lay their plans accordingly. Another
disadvantage to European troops in South Africa
is that European horses do not naturally take to

South African pasture, and that there are poisonous
plants to be found in it which native horses have
learned to avoid, but which European horses will
innocently devour. Hence forage becomes a great
difficulty also ; and on the veldt there is the further
drawback that no wood for fuel exists. As in most
new lands, the roads are mere tracks, and all the
innumerable rivers must be crossed by fords, for
there are few bridges; while the extent of the territory
that may be covered by military operations in so
vast a continent is appalling.

In one of our earliest Kaffir wars—that of 1835—
Sir Harry Smith described himself as having only
twelve hundred men, eight hundred horses and four
guns, with which to act in a theatre of war of four
thousand square miles ; and he added, " It takes just
two hours for a commissariat train to arrive, from the
moving off of the first waggon to the arrival of the
last, when the road is good. When the column is
stretched out along the road it looks as if each soldier
had a waggon to himself at least." Yet on one occasion with a small force he marched eighty-four miles
in three days ; and he covered nearly two hundred and
twenty miles in a rugged and mountainous country,
much broken by deep rivers, in seven days and a half.
In the more serious war of 1850–53 the hostile tribes
could not put into the field more than three thousand
fighting men ; but by betaking themselves to their

fastnesses of mountain and forest they prolonged their resistance for nearly three years. The British soldier was at every disadvantage in bush-fighting, and the Kaffirs were far too cunning to encounter him in the open; yet by dint of hard work and perseverance this brave and wary enemy was at last worn down. He might have been subdued much earlier but for the constant and insane reductions of the Army ever since Waterloo. It is actually a fact that at this time the military power of England was strained almost to breaking point by three thousand naked savages.

The next war—that of 1877—came at a time when our Army, owing to the recent introduction of short service, was in a state of transition, and taught us a very severe lesson. We were engaged in war with the Zulus, a very formidable tribe, which had been organised into a great military power by a chief who, in his own way, was a genius. One of his armies came upon a British force of something over a thousand troops at a disadvantage, and after a desperate fight destroyed them almost to a man. But for the determined resistance of a small post of eighty or ninety men at a ford of the Tugela, the Zulus would probably have overrun Natal to the sea, and extinguished the white inhabitants of that Colony. There was great agitation in England, and several battalions were hurried out to the Cape with no special regard to their condition or quality. It had been forgotten that the old long-service-soldier had become extinct ; and that the old single-battalion-regiments were also in course of extinction, to give place to regiments of two battalions, whereof one was always to be at home and the other abroad. The Army and the nation had not taken kindly to the change ; and the immediate result was that the battalions at home had become merely assemblies of boys who, as soon as they approached manhood, were drafted off to feed the battalions abroad. Some of these groups of boys, raw and half-trained, were shipped out to South Africa in the expectation that they would be as strong and as steady as the old battalions composed of men who counted ten to twenty years' service. Of course they were not. They were very sickly, very ill-disciplined, and very far from well-conducted. However, the war was ended, and the power of the Zulus was broken without further serious mishap ; and we learned by this experience the lesson that a force of seasoned soldiers must at all times be held ready for what is called the police-work of the Empire.

Our last experience of war in South Africa is too recent for me to presume to say much about it, except that in many respects it bore a singular resemblance to the American War of Independence. The operations of the latter war embraced at least eleven

hundred miles of coast-line, as the crow flies, and in
places penetrated inland as far as a hundred and fifty
miles from the sea. Only facilities of water-carriage
enabled armies to be moved at all over this vast
tract ; and it was rare for bodies even of ten thousand
men to remain for long united. The theatre of war
in South Africa was quite as vast. Our two principal bases of operations were nearly a thousand miles
apart—as far, say, as Antwerp is from Lisbon, with
the enemy's capital situated at Warsaw. But for
the existence of a few railways the conquest of this
enormous tract might have taken thirty years, for
there are no waterways and the country produces
little wheat. As things were, it was accomplished
more or less in three ; and a force of three to four
hundred thousand men was fed with a regularity
highly creditable to the officers responsible for that
duty. But the expense was terrific ; and although
it was possible by great exertions to bring up food
for the men, there were moments when it was impossible to provide sufficient forage for the animals.
Hence the waste of horses in the cavalry and artillery
was enormous, for they could not live on the African
pasture as did the horses of the enemy. In fact a
community with a more or less empty continent at
its back can, with good management, prolong resistance for an almost indefinite time ; for the chances
are that the invader will be more quickly exhausted

than the invaded, while the former is always subject
to troubles and diversions at home which may
weaken him at a critical moment. That is the
secret of the power of Russia and of the United
States. It is impossible to hurt them seriously, for
the further you penetrate into their country the
weaker you are. Little countries, such as our own,
may be pierced to the heart at the first thrust.
Space in fact means time where war is concerned ;
and time is the most powerful of all allies. The
Americans themselves discovered that when they
invaded Canada in 1812.

There is another description of colonial war of
which we have had experience, and which from
the extreme peculiarity of the country and people
deserves special notice. I speak of New Zealand.
Roughly speaking the two main islands of New
Zealand exactly correspond to Italy in our own
hemisphere ; and if you suppose the sea to close
round the northern frontier of the Alps and to cut
the peninsula in two by washing a channel through
it somewhere about Rome, you will find the actual
shape of New Zealand very closely reproduced.
Both countries consist of a backbone of volcanic
mountains, with a broad margin to east and a narrow
margin to west ; and in each there is a wide
fertile plain made up of débris washed down from the
mountains and furrowed by rivers flowing from the

glaciers. This great plain, however, is in the south island of New Zealand ; and all of our wars were in the north island, corresponding in the southern hemisphere to the southern portion of Italy. The north island, which contains several active volcanoes, is for the most part mountainous and was to a vast extent covered with dense forest, with a strong undergrowth of vines—known as supple-jacks—and of fern, very like our own bracken, which grows higher than a man's head. The inhabitants were themselves invaders from the North Pacific, or possibly from some part of the American continent, and, according to their own traditions, must have occupied the country at about the time of our own Norman Conquest. They were called, as of course you know, by the name of Maoris, and were split up into a number of tribes which passed their time in continual warfare with each other, and hence possessed some degree of military organisation. Their weapons and tools were made of stone, the best of them of jade. With such tools they had skill to build canoes and art to ornament both prow and paddle with not unbeautiful carving. They were cannibals, for the simple reason that they could get no other meat ; for until the white man came there were no four-footed creatures in the two islands— nothing but birds. They caught and dried fish, however, and had little provision-grounds of potatoes.

But their chief business, as I have said, was fighting ; and they were a fine athletic and high-spirited race. For the rest they had a natural gift of fortification. They needed no great talent to select good positions in so hilly a country where natural strongholds abound ; but they showed great skill in throwing up tiers of earth-works and erecting stockades of trees a foot in diameter, tightly bound together with supple-jacks.

The first white men came to them in the form of whaling skippers, who initiated them into the use of fire-arms, and sold such weapons as they could spare to one or two chiefs. The remaining tribes soon discovered that, if they were to escape extermination, they must obtain fire-arms also ; and thus there grew up a large trade in arms and ammunition for which the Maoris paid in native flax—*phormium tenax*—laboriously scraped with shells till only the tough fibre was left, and of supreme excellence from this careful method of curing. Two-barrelled fowling pieces—*tuparas* as they called them—were the favourite weapon, and the Maoris soon became expert in their use ; adding thereupon rifle-pits and covered trenches to their fortifications to meet attack with the new weapon. Incidentally this natural craze for fire-arms materially injured the race, for, in order to scrape flax enough to pay for them, the whole tribe was obliged to come down

from the hill-tops and live by the swamps where the
phormium tenax grows and abounds.

How we came into collision with the Maoris, who
had frequently received white men—deserting sailors
and such like—into their tribes with much friendli-
ness, is not a pretty story ; being only one of the
many variations on the old theme of the white man's
greed for the black man's property. Of course it
was necessary to send troops out ; and our commanders, hearing of the fortifications or *pas* erected by
the Maoris, thought that such works could not have
been thrown up except to defend something, and
that it would be desirable to capture them. They
therefore brought up a gun or two with infinite
labour, and after firing a certain number of rounds,
let loose their assaulting columns to the attack.
Now as a matter of fact the Maoris built their *pas*
upon no such principle ; and the loss of a *pa* was
nothing to them so long as no life was lost with it.
They therefore continued to build *pas* in the hope that
the white men would ram their heads against them ;
and they did so with considerable cunning, erecting
their first *pa* close to the edge of the forest, retiring
from that to a second further within the woods,
so as to lure the English deeper and deeper into
disadvantageous ground, and from that in turn to
a third. By the time the third was reached the
English were unable to bring their food any further,

and, having lost heavily in their assaults, were fain
to retire and await reinforcements.

The chief difficulty, as in all savage campaigns,
lay of course in transport and supply. There were
no roads or bridges, and few animals, whether horses,
mules or cattle ; but as all the settlements were on
the sea, the Maoris had built their *pas* in the vicinity,
so as to be ready to attack the whites at any moment.
Still, even when the difficulty of transport and supply
was overcome, our commanders were greatly puzzled
how to injure the Maoris. So powerfully were the
tree-trunks of a stockade laced together, that even
when broken by a shot they did not fall, but remained
suspended, a nasty if not impossible obstacle, by
the binders of supple-jack. Thus assaults were
always costly, and somehow the Maori garrison
always contrived to escape. Again and again a
pa was surrounded, but there was always a ravine or
a watercourse by which the Maoris slipped away ;
and when the British column, maddened by heavy
losses, broke into the earth-works, it was to find
no one there. Once two British columns stormed
a *pa*, enduring heavy fire until they reached the
summit, when the Maoris dived down into their
subterranean galleries. The British soldiers, rushing
in from opposite sides, met at the top, and poured
a staggering volley into each other, whereupon up
came the Maoris from underground, and sent the

assailants flying down again in panic. Altogether
the problem of the *pa* seemed to be insoluble, for the
galleries and rifle-pits of the Maoris were so cunning-
ly constructed that a bombardment inflicted only
trifling damage on them. Critics at a distance wrote
that every success (for such the capture of a *pa*
was deemed to be) should be followed by a rapid
advance into the forest. But deep ravines and
gullies covered either with a network of supple-jacks,
or with fallen logs and trees hidden in bracken six
or seven feet high, is not ground over which men
can advance rapidly. I know it because I have tried
it ; and the unhappy soldiers, who had also tried
it, waxed furious over the ignorant presumption of
those who talked such nonsense.

At last it occurred to a British officer that the
Maoris wished their *pas* to be assaulted, and that
they considered it a victory when several scores of
British fell in an attack upon a worthless stronghold,
while the defenders quietly retired with at most two
or three casualties. And this was the fact. Having
grasped this truth the officer determined not to
attack them ; but marched up to the vicinity of a
pa, sat down in front of it, and entrenched himself
and his guns before it. This did not suit the Maoris
at all. They saw that they would be obliged to
go back sooner or later, without the satisfaction of
killing fifty or sixty of the enemy, and they did not

see where the process might end. In desperation they attempted several attacks against the English earth-works, but were repulsed with heavy loss, and were fain to draw back to another *pa* further within the forest. The British followed, and went through the same performance again, with the same result. In a few weeks these particular Maoris gave in, for they saw no prospect of emerging from the forest again ; and though they might have kept themselves alive on fern-root, they knew that their warriors would soon lose all physical strength upon such a diet. The Maori wars lasted in one way or another for nearly twenty years in a desultory fashion, partly owing to mismanagement, partly, I fear, because so many contractors in the colonial towns made money out of them that people were unwilling to let them come to an end. When the Imperial troops and money were withdrawn, and the colonists were left to finish the job for themselves, the trouble with the Maoris soon ceased.

Lastly we come to those expeditions which even in these days tend to be most dangerous and costly, I mean those to such fever-stricken coasts as the Gold Coast and the Delta of the Congo, where all supplies and stores must be carried on the heads of men and women, and where even the strictest care may fail to avert deadly sickness. Twice within forty years has a British force marched to Coomassie ;

but the wise tendency nowadays is to entrust such work almost exclusively to native troops who do not suffer from the climate. The number of these troops has increased enormously of late years with the extension of our rule in Africa ; and we are accustomed to treat the fact as a matter of course, without a thought for the man who has made these foreign levies what they are, and without whom they are nothing—the British officer.

I have sketched for you very briefly the rise of the Empire, and now at the close of this third lecture I am going to say a word for the man who has had the chief share in winning it—the British regimental officer. It is the fashion in some circles to belittle him ; and the press, in the plenitude of its ignorance, took occasion during the South African War to cover him with vulgar abuse, reproaching him for his ignorance of his profession and various other short-comings. As a matter of fact he was the one man in South Africa who understood his business, and it was he who brought the war to a successful con-clusion. In these days of democracy, so-called, it is common to vituperate, concurrently with the officer, the English public schools where he obtained his education. Neither officers nor public schools make any reply to such criticisms ; and they are quite right, for the British Empire is a sufficient reply to the critics, who are fonder of framing theories than of studying hard facts. I am not saying that our public schools are perfect, for in many respects they seem to me very faulty ; nor shall I contend that the men who spring from them are, in the ordinary sense of the term, educated, for they are not. The German *gymnasium* and French Lycée undoubtedly produce men who are better schooled to the study of books, and more amply filled with a certain description of facts. But at any rate the pupils from our public schools become men who, after a certain amount of military training, do not shrink from command, and are willing to take responsibility. In brief, they are formed in character if not cultivated in intellect ; they are not ignorant of men, whatever they may be of books ; and they are willing to undertake the government of men, not from mere lust of power, but from instinctive delight in the task.

It is curious how often people complain of the ignorance and narrowness of young officers, saying that they can think of nothing outside their regiments, unless it be polo or some other game in which the regiment is interested. No doubt it is better for men of any profession to know something, and the more the better, of subjects outside that profession ; and yet what could more profitably occupy an officer's thoughts than the men and horses under his charge ? Military routine can have no doubt a somewhat straitening and deadening

effect upon officers, even as academic routine may
injuriously affect the minds of schoolmasters and
professors ; and no doubt there are officers who chafe
under it.   But the majority find more than sufficient
interest in the study of their men, in the selection
of the promising for promotion, the encouragement
of the good, the improvement, suppression and elim-
ination of the bad, the bringing on of the backward,
and above all in honest endeavour to enter into the
thoughts of their men—a task so difficult that not
one in ten thousand succeeds in mastering it.   For
they know that it is their business to lead men and
not drive them to discipline, and to inspire such
confidence between commanded and commander that
even in the most desperate situation he may be able
to say, *I can depend upon my men.*

But even those who tire of military routine in
time of peace change their opinion when they go
upon active service.   In England they cannot see
why all kinds of tiresome details should not be left
to the sergeants, but in the field they soon discover
that the men will listen to and trust no one but
an officer.   The non-commissioned officer does not
suffice for them.   He may be a veteran of eighteen
years' service ; but the men will follow a commis-
sioned boy of eighteen fresh from Eton infinitely
more readily than they will the non-commissioned
veteran.   It is a very remarkable fact, and to those

who hold that all men are equal it is extremely
unpalatable ; but a fact beyond question it is, and
not difficult of explanation. Men who by the fortune
of their birth are exempted from the bitterness of
the struggle for existence, trust their fellows because
they have no reason to dread their competition ;
men who have been brought up in the thick of the
fight with none but themselves to help them, see a
possible competitor—it may be even a dangerous
enemy—in every neighbour, and trust no one.

Yet active service is by no means necessary to
cure the officer who is bored with military service
at home. Send him away to some outlandish corner
of the Empire, and entrust him with the training and
command of a few hundred black soldiers, and he
will find exile, hardship and discomfort more congenial to him in such company than the softest of
lives at home. He realises that everything, so far
as those few hundred men are concerned, depends
upon himself ; and he delights in the sensation.
There are hundreds of such officers in remote places
quietly doing what some consider the dirty work,
but what they themselves know to be the most
honourable work, of the Empire. The officers of the
Indian Army are in precisely the same case. Few
of us realise how much we owe to them, and to how
great an extent the Empire is dependent upon them.
Operatives in our huge over-grown towns, who exhaust

themselves in condemnation of everything military, never reflect that, but for this handful of officers, their comrades of the Indian Army, and the disciplined men, Indian too, but above all British, who serve under them, millions of themselves who subsist upon our trade with India would be in a state of starvation. Happily the officers, and therefore the men who serve under them, do their duty patiently and quietly without regarding the volumes of chatter which flow unceasingly from the north country ; for they know that empires are won and governed not by talk but by action.

This, I think, is a thing that we should all do well to remember from time to time. Exaggerated esteem for our Parliamentary institutions has led us to attach too much importance to speeches. Their original purpose was to persuade men to a common course of action ; but they have never been very efficacious, and in this country have long been superseded by political organisation or, in plain English, wire-pulling. People have a strange notion that, without much chatter, there can be no liberty. But liberty (whatever liberty may be) is a small thing to a nation compared with discipline ; and in fact liberty of any kind is impossible without discipline. If I am to judge of a nation it is useless to tell me of its political institutions, for the best of them will work badly and the worst of them well according to the honesty of the men whose business it is to apply them. Let me know what is the state of its discipline, parental, social, national, and with what spirit that discipline is borne. Let me know what are its military institutions, and how far they are supported or ignored; whether the citizens come forward with cheerfulness to fulfil a national duty, or whether they are reckless, self-indulgent shirkers who try to impose on a few the service that is common to all, and take refuge in cant to disguise their cowardice. Then I will tell you without reading a single speech whether the nation is sound at heart or rotten. If the text of all the speeches ever delivered in Parliament were destroyed to-morrow, the world would lose remarkably little. Great men are best studied in their letters and their actions, whether they were great speakers or not; and by no means the worst way of appreciating the actions of very many of them, both civilians and soldiers, is to read military history.

LECTURE IV

BRITISH CAMPAIGNS IN INDIA

TO-DAY I propose to speak to you upon a very great and most intractable subject—British Military History in India. It is difficult to do so without saying something of the history of India itself ; yet the subject is so immense that I must compress the whole of that vast story into one or two sentences.

Let me begin then by reminding you that what we call India is divided into a northern portion, which extends from the Himalayas southward to the Narbada river and the Vindhya Mountains and is called Hindostan ; and a southern portion called the Dekhan which stretches from those boundaries southward to Cape Comorin. This division is less arbitrary than a glance at the map would lead you to suppose ; for between these two huge territories there lies a belt of barren and mountainous country, through which, before the days of railways, there was practically but one passage, famous in Indian military history as the Ajanta Pass. The earliest invaders of whom we have any knowledge came by sea, and landing in the extreme south worked their way from thence to the northern boundary of the Dekhan. The people of the Dekhan still speak the language of these invaders, which is unknown in Hindostan. The next invaders, the Aryans, came through the passes of Afghanistan from the north-west, bringing with them the religious and social institutions which are known to us as Hinduism, Brahminism and caste, and which still govern the lives of most of the millions who now inhabit Hindostan. They penetrated, however, only into one corner of the Dekhan—the north-west—where the Aryan language, Marathi, betrays their presence.

I pass over the innumerable tides of invasion which swept over Hindostan from the north-west, until we come to the first formidable inroad of Mohammedan Arabs in 999 A.D. The great champions of Hinduism against Islam were the Rajputs, whose nobles still represent the highest aristocracy and the bluest blood in India. For a long time they combated desperately and with success; but in 1193 the Mohammedans captured Delhi, and within another twenty years they definitely overthrew the Rajputs and established themselves as potential masters of India. For Delhi, though the maps do not show it, is a great strategical position, marking the centre of a kind of pass, where the access to India from the north-west is narrowed to a tract, not above one hundred miles broad, between the mountains on the north and a desert on the south. Hence all the decisive battles of India against invaders from the north-west have been fought within fifty miles of Delhi.

In the fifteenth century a new set of Mohammedan invaders—the Turkis or Tartars—came down
upon the Arabs, and after more than a hundred
years of raiding, invaded Hindostan in good earnest
under a great leader, Baber. In 1526 they became
masters of Delhi. Then for two hundred years
strong man succeeded strong man, and there was
consolidated what is called the Mogul Empire.
Akbar, one of the great men of all time, reigned
from 1556 until 1605—almost exactly the period of
our own Elizabeth—and gathered all India north of
the Narbada, from Kandahar to the Bay of Bengal,
into a single Empire. His successors strove hard,
though with indifferent results, to subjugate the
Dekhan; but by the middle of the seventeenth
century signs of decay were evident among the
Moguls. The Hindus, whether warriors as the
Rajputs, or meek and submissive, as the Bengalis,
have an amazing power of silently and gradually
absorbing all alien races into themselves. At this
moment a sharp line divides Mohammedans from
Hindus; and yet the Mohammedans have already
caught the system of caste from the Hindus, and
as centuries roll on will doubtless be more and more
drawn into the likeness of the Hindus, until the
two races are indistinguishable. Intermarriage con-
tributes greatly to this; and it was intermarriage
with Hindu women, and the consequent dilution

of the stern Tartar blood, which weakened and
ruined the Mogul Emperors.

The last eminent man of the line, Aurungzib,
perhaps inspired by the deterioration of his country-
men, was a rabid Mohammedan fanatic, so relent-
less in his persecutions that he raised up a host of
enemies and brought about the ruin of the Mogul
Empire. The Rajputs reappeared as the champions
of Hinduism, but there also came forward two new
defenders. The first may be described as a Puritan
sect, the Sikhs. They were at the outset only
martyrs, but later, when a man of genius was born
among them, they became in the nineteenth century
a great military power. The second and more important were the Marathas, the followers of Sivaji
Bonsla, a petty chief from the hills above Bombay,
who being a fine military leader, wore out the armies
of Aurungzib by what we call guerilla tactics. What
the Marathas were no one can say. They were not
a caste, nor a sect, nor a nation; but they were a
homogeneous body, and they would, but for us
English, have become the masters of India.

Our own start in India was humble; but the
East India Company began in the early years of
the seventeenth century to establish factories, or
trading depots, at various points on the coast, including one at Madras in 1640 and on the Hugli in
1651. Bombay, which was part of the dowry of

Katharine of Bragança, was leased to the Company in 1661, and Calcutta was founded in 1690. But all the factories suffered much during the incessant fighting between Sivaji and Aurungzib; and the Company in 1686 declared its intention of making reprisals. It had already formed the nuclei of European armies in Madras in 1644 and in Bombay in 1668; and had begun to enlist native troops in 1683. But meanwhile another European power, the French, had established factories in Madras at Pondicherry and in Bengal at Chandernagore in the year 1674; and the progress of events was such as to offer great temptation to foreign adventurers. Aurungzib died in 1707, and with the passing of the last strong man the realm of the Moguls crumbled rapidly away. The viceroy of the Dekhan set himself up as an independent sovereign at Haiderabad; a Hindu dynasty was founded at Tanjore; another imperial official seized Oude; one adventurer laid hold of Bengal; another of Rohilkhand; countless soldiers of fortune planted themselves as petty chieftains in hill-fortresses; a Persian invader sacked Delhi; and an Afghan chieftain conquered the whole of the western Punjab. India had never been in a more appalling welter of confusion and chaos than in the midst of the eighteenth century.

Just at this period the English and French for

the first time came to blows in the Peninsula, the
pretext being the war of the Austrian Succession.
The French, represented at Pondicherry by a very
able agent, Dupleix, had initiated a policy of diplomatic interference in the affairs of the neighbouring
states, having an army of seven thousand Sepoys to
back them. The British on the other hand stuck
to their trading, and, as usual, were unprepared for
any attack. The French therefore besieged and
took Madras in 1746 ; but, being reinforced in time,
the British in turn besieged but did not take
Pondicherry. The Peace of Aix-la-Chapelle followed,
which put an end to hostilities ; and Madras was
restored to us in exchange for Louisburg. The
most significant incident of the war, however, was
that the Nawab of the Carnatic, the nominal suzerain of both the English and the French on the
Coromandel coast, had attempted to keep the peace
between them ; and that his raw levies, to the
number of ten thousand, had been swept off the
field in five minutes by two hundred and fifty
French soldiers and thrice that number of trained
Sepoys. This showed that a handful of disciplined
European soldiers could suffice to rout any primitive
Oriental host. Another important matter was that
the operations against the French had revealed a
remarkable leader in the British ranks, namely
Major Stringer Lawrence, a simple man who could

hardly write his name, but a fine soldier and a judge
of men. For he selected from the counting-house
of the Company a young clerk named Robert Clive,
took his military education in hand, and to all
intents adopted him as his son.

Meanwhile the death of the Nawab of the Carnatic
and of the Viceroy of the Dekhan almost simultaneously gave Dupleix an opportunity, which he
did not neglect, of making French influence paramount at both Courts. The succession, as almost
invariably happens in the East, was disputed ; and
Dupleix, by supporting in each case one candidate,
saw his way to making him a puppet and himself
the actual ruler. The English of course supported
the rival candidates ; and thus, though France and
England were at peace, the representatives of both
nations in India were at war as auxiliaries of native
princes. Stringer Lawrence being at home on leave,
English military affairs went sadly wrong ; and at
one moment the situation was so desperate that
it was only saved by a diversion against Arcot, the
capital of the Carnatic, by the young but not
uninstructed volunteer Clive. However in 1752
Lawrence returned, and in that and the following
year he gained victory after victory over the French.
The centre of the fighting, by a singular chain of
accidents, was the city of Trichinopoly ; and in the
plain before it Lawrence, with forces ranging from

eight hundred to three thousand regular troops, two-thirds of them Sepoys, against superior numbers of French, fought a series of beautiful little actions, out-manœuvring his enemy on the open ground by what would now be called parade movements, but which were then the finest achievements of training and discipline. In 1754 Dupleix was recalled to France to answer for misconduct, and the struggle was closed by a suspension of arms. The interest of these few years, 1748 to 1754, is that, France and England being at peace, their fleets could not intervene in the contest; otherwise the power which enjoyed supremacy at sea was bound to win, being always able to bring out her own reinforcements and exclude those of the enemy. When the fight was resumed, the influence of superiority at sea was very clearly seen; but meanwhile the year 1753 had witnessed a new departure in British policy in India, namely the arrival of a king's regiment, the 39th Dorsetshire, which still bears the motto *Primus in Indis*. Henceforward the rivalry in the great peninsula was not to be between trading companies but between nations.

And now you will ask what manner of campaigns were these ? I must answer that generally speaking they were extremely comfortable. The theatre of war, which extended along about two hundred miles of the east coast from Madras to the River Cavery, and about fifty miles inland, is mostly easy country, cultivated and full of supplies, with abundance of old fortified places to serve for depots and magazines. Thus the sea could be used for the conveyance of troops and heavy stores along the coast (though the ports are unsafe during the monsoon) ; while inland there was abundance of native carts and of bullocks, which, though small and weakly, could travel at the rate of two miles an hour. The army was, as always in India, accompanied by a vast number of followers—in those days about ten followers to one fighting man, though the proportion has now been greatly reduced. In fact an army on the march had much the appearance of a moving city, every kind of trade, profession and calling being represented, with speculators, in particular, in great strength. On the march the officers were for the most part carried in palanquins, and they were of course attended by the full strength of their native households, with every appliance for their comfort. The men marched, the British, so far as one can gather, in full European costume and with no special protection from the sun ; though it is difficult to be certain about the matter, for it is quite likely that they were equipped very much according to the notions of their officers. They too had plenty of followers to look after them. The Sepoys, so far as uniform went, were dressed in a short red jacket, a curious semi-oriental, semi-European black head-dress, very short little white drawers barely reaching mid-thigh, and native shoes. The Madrassi is not a fighting man—indeed Lord Roberts went so far as to disband most of the true Madras infantry—and it is almost certain that the sepoys who fought with Lawrence, Clive, Coote, and Wellesley were adventurers from all parts of India, including many from the fighting races of the north. The British in column of route marched two abreast, the Sepoys three abreast, for though well disciplined their drill was primitive ; and, so far as I can gather, they knew few words of command (apart from the manual and firing exercise) except " Right turn " and " Left turn," which sufficed to bring them from line into column and from column into line, the British in two ranks, the Sepoys in three. It must be added that the Company's troops, being accustomed to march from place to place to relieve each other in various garrisons, always kept a respectable amount of transport with them, and hence could enter upon a campaign ready mobilised. But at all times the number of the followers was, and still is, a great encumbrance, and, when supplies and forage were scanty, an appalling difficulty.

So much for Madras ; but Madras was only one of three presidencies, which were practically as far from each other as England is from Portugal. From

Calcutta to Madras is a good eight hundred miles
by sea ; and by land the journey was almost impracticable owing to the number of great rivers
that cross the line of march.   From Bombay to the
British settlements on the Malabar coast is another
eight hundred miles by sea, and to Madras itself,
going round Ceylon, over two thousand miles.   From
Calcutta to Bombay overland is a thousand miles as
the crow flies, though part of the distance could be
traversed by river, and by sea at least two thousand
five hundred miles.   Moreover there was until 1773
no Governor-General ; but the three presidencies
of Bombay, Bengal and Madras were co-equal, and
divided moreover by jealousies and self-importance.

The opening of the Seven Years' War in 1756
brought about a renewal of hostilities ; but it began
with an unexpected disaster in the capture of Calcutta, through a sudden fit of jealousy, by Siraj-ud-
Daula, the Nawab of Bengal.   Upon this disaster
followed the tragedy of the Black Hole.   It was
necessary to send troops up from Madras under
Clive to recover the city with all haste, for French
reinforcements were expected at Pondicherry, and
there was no fleet to stop them.   Having but a
handful of men, Clive contrived to detach one of
the Nawab's principal officers from him, and by
the man's treacherous assistance defeated Siraj-ud-
Daula at Plassey.   This done, he installed Mir

Jaffier, the officer aforesaid, in the Nawab's place, and left a young clerk named Warren Hastings to keep him in order.

Meanwhile a very able French officer, one de Bussy, had contrived by consummate skill and daring to restore French influence with the Viceroy of the Dekhan, but, having little military force at his command, was unable to effect much, while the British themselves were too weak greatly to harm their enemies. In the spring of 1758 the French reinforcements arrived, and the commander, Count Lally Tollendal, was able to take the field with twenty-five hundred Europeans—an enormous force in those days—and half as many Sepoys. He captured several minor places in the first few months, but, finding himself short of money, turned southward to take some from the rich Rajah of Mysore. Persecuting and bullying wherever he went, he soon turned all the natives against him. All cattle were driven off, all food was hidden away ; and, when Tanjore was reached, he found himself opposed not only by natives but by part of the British garrison of Trichinopoly, which the British commandant had sent to their assistance. After heavy loss and much suffering he returned to Pondicherry, where he learned that after a sharp action the French fleet had been driven from the coast by a British fleet of inferior numbers ; and, what with one trouble and

another, it was December before he could lay siege
to Madras. He stayed before the city for two
months, when the appearance of the British fleet,
which had been refitted after the recent engagement,
compelled him to retreat. Meanwhile Clive in
Bengal had detached a small force, as a diversion,
by sea against the French settlements in the Northern
Sirkars, about two hundred miles north of Madras ;
where the commander, Colonel Forde of the Thirty-
ninth, fought a brilliant campaign against superior
numbers, and by his success not only extinguished
the French power in that quarter but banished
French influence in favour of English at the court
of the Viceroy of the Dekhan. The tide now turned.
Fresh reinforcements arrived from England together
with a new commander, Colonel Eyre Coote, to take
the place of Lawrence whose health had given way.
The Dutch in Batavia, always jealous of the British,
fitted out an expedition to attack their rivals in
Bengal while the bulk of British troops were in
Madras ; but it was useless. Clive detached Forde
with orders to fight them immediately. Forde did
so, overthrowing their superior numbers in half an
hour, and capturing their army almost to a man.
Three months later Coote met Lally at Wandewash
upon equal terms and completely defeated him, thus
destroying for ever the French competition for the
mastery of India.

While the British power was thus growing, that
of the Marathas had increased likewise ; and they
had organised themselves into a confederacy of
five co-equal parts under five principal chiefs.   In
1758 their success ran so high that they laid hold
upon Delhi itself ; but this was too much for the
Mohammedan Afghans.   They came down in their
wrath ; and in 1761 a great battle was fought at
Panipat in which the Marathas were utterly defeated.
Had the Afghans followed up their success, the
Marathas would have taken long to recover from
the blow ; but the victors were obliged to look to
their own western frontier which was threatened
by the Persians ; and the only result of the fight
was to exhaust two of the possible masters of
northern India and leave the country in greater
confusion than ever.   Most unfortunately, too, Clive,
the representative of the third possible master,
went home on leave at this time ; and the supreme
power in Bengal passed into the hands of the Company's clerks.   Having no high standard before
their eyes and being miserably paid, these clerks
saw the chance of enriching themselves by selling
the use of the Company's troops to any potentate
or adventurer who might offer to buy ; and, by
setting up and throwing down the Nawabs of Bengal
as best suited their pockets, they involved the
Company in most perilous and soon disastrous

wars. From the worst of their difficulties they
were extricated by the military genius of Major
Thomas Adams, who though deficient alike in men,
arms and supplies, contrived by three victories at
Katwa, Suti and Undwa Nala in July, August and
September, 1763, to maintain the terror of the
British arms. But the titular Emperor of Delhi
of the Mogul dynasty also entered the fray, and
strove with the help of the Nawab of Oudh to re-
establish his former sovereignty over Bengal ; and
to make matters worse at this critical moment there
was a mutiny among the Sepoys of the Bengal
Presidency. The mutiny, however, was sternly
repressed by Major Hector Munro, who then led
his army against the Emperor and utterly defeated
him at Buxar on the 23rd of February, 1764. This
victory opened the way to Oudh, and the British
captured in succession the great cities of Allahabad
and Lucknow ; when at this moment Clive returned
and stopped further annexation. He had no wish
to have for neighbours the adventurers who had
sprung up at Delhi, Agra, Bhurtpore and in Rohilkhand. He therefore restored Oudh to its Nawab,
so as to keep it a buffer-state between Bengal and
the rest of Hindostan.

In Madras likewise the British officials had
lost their heads. They were threatened by two
dangerous enemies, the Marathas, and Hyder Ali,

a Mohammedan soldier who by sheer military genius had acquired the sovereignty of Mysore, and from that base was threatening the territory alike of the Marathas, the Nizam, and the British in southern India. The British might have played off their rivals against each other, but they contrived instead to make enemies of both; and Hyder Ali was a formidable opponent. Happily there was a British officer, Colonel Joseph Smith, who was more than his equal, and before whom Hyder trembled in the field. But the Council of Madras displaced Smith to make room for a creature of their own; and the consequence was that in 1769 Hyder Ali advanced to within five miles of Madras itself, and forced the Council to an humiliating peace. Even so, however, though they obtained the mercy, they did not obtain the forgiveness of the ruler of Mysore.

In 1773 the British Parliament passed an Act which, among other reforms, made the Governor of Bengal the Governor-General of all three provinces, but most foolishly omitted to make him supreme in his own Council, leaving him instead at the mercy of the majority. Warren Hastings was the first Governor-General, and well for us it is that he was so; for no smaller man would have sufficed to preserve our dominion in India against the folly and malignity of the adverse faction in his Council. He made of his own will but one war, against the

predatory Rohillas, whom he compelled to pay
due obedience to their suzerain the Nawab of Oudh.
This action was afterwards distorted by the malignity of his enemies into a crime. But the Government of Bombay, like those of Madras and Bengal,
had through greed of territory entangled itself in
a war with the Marathas ; and Hastings, while
utterly disapproving its policy, found it imperative
to send assistance. Moreover, he had the courage
to order the reinforcements to march overland from
the frontier of Oudh to Bombay, a thing which
hitherto had never been dreamed of ; and indeed
the passage of six battalions of Sepoys across
Hindostan over a vast extent of territory which no
Englishman knew and where no one could say
whether they would be welcomed or fired upon, is
a sufficiently striking episode. Unfortunately the
commander allowed himself to be tempted to do a
little fighting for some petty potentates on the way ;
and this delay caused Hastings's heroic determina-
tion to be in great measure fruitless. The Bombay
Government too managed its military affairs so ill
that no operations of their designing could prosper ;
and finally it was necessary to patch up a hasty and
discreditable peace with the Marathas in the north-
west in view of a far more formidable danger else-
where.

For in 1778, as will be remembered, the French

declared war upon us in consequence of our disasters
in America ; and in 1780 Hyder Ali, the southern
Marathas and the Nizam formed a confederacy to
expel the British from India. In June of that year
Hyder descended from Mysore upon Madras with
ninety thousand men, including four hundred French,
and fifteen thousand Sepoys trained and disciplined
after the European manner. The wretched Council of
Madras had nothing ready, neither men, nor stores,
nor supplies ; and unfortunately Hector Munro of
Buxar, who held the command of such troops as
there were, managed his affairs badly and divided
his force. One detachment of three thousand men
was cut to pieces ; and matters were so serious
that Hastings sent Sir Eyre Coote down to take
command in the Carnatic, with every soldier that
could be spared from Bengal. A superior French
fleet was on the coast, and Hyder conceived the
bold notion of capturing or destroying all supplies
that Coote might use ashore, while the French cut
off all that might arrive by sea. Happily the French
admiral left the coast in the nick of time to save
Coote, who averted all immediate danger by the
victory of Porto Novo ; but in the campaign that
followed the British general was so much hampered
by Hyder's light troops that he could hardly keep
the field from want of transport and supplies.
Another mishap then occurred ; and a detachment

of a thousand British troops was surprised and cut
to pieces; while a succession of naval actions left
the French fleet practically supreme on the coast.
Hyder Ali died early in 1782, and Eyre Coote soon
followed him, but Hyder's son Tippoo was an abler
man than Coote's successor. In 1783 the crisis
came. A detachment of a thousand men from
Bombay, which had been sent to make a diversion
on the west side of Mysore, was cut off and captured
by Tippoo; and a month later a formidable French
force landed at Cuddalore (Gadalur) on the east
coast, and fought a severe though indecisive action
against the British under General Stuart. Three
days later the French squadron on the coast under
Admiral Suffren drove off the British ships and
landed yet more reinforcements, which gave them
a decided superiority over the British. The fate
of British supremacy in India hung in the balance
for seven anxious days, when in the nick of time
news came that peace had been concluded between
France and England in Europe. So nearly were
all the victories of Lawrence, Clive and Eyre Coote
neutralised by incompetent administration at Bombay and Madras. The one able man among Indian
officials, Warren Hastings, went home to be shamefully persecuted under the form of a judicial trial by
a clique of vindictive politicians. They succeeded
in ruining him financially by sheer blackguardly

cunning; but they could not damage his great name, which will never be forgotten in India while British rule endures.

Parliament now amended the government of India by giving the Governor-General absolute and supreme power, and making the chief officials responsible to Parliament instead of to the Company. These were good and useful reforms; but extreme anxiety to check the levying of war for purposes of gain led English statesmen to enact further that the Governor-General should not make war at all except for defence, thus leaving to his enemies practically the undisputed power of taking the initiative in hostilities. Lord Cornwallis, a good soldier, was the first Governor-General under the new system; and Tippoo Sahib at once took advantage of it to make a raid into the Carnatic. Cornwallis accordingly took the field against him in 1791, and invaded Mysore from the east, while a detachment from Bombay invaded it from the west. The enterprise was most difficult, for it was certain that, as soon as the British arrived on the table-land of Mysore, Tippoo would draw a ring of devastation about them, destroying all food and forage. With enormous difficulty Cornwallis reached Seringapatam, Tippoo's capital city, and laid siege to it; but, strive as he would, he could not provide transport for more than twenty days' supplies, and

he could only bring forward his ammunition by
paying the women and boys among the followers to
carry each a cannon-shot or two.   Before he reached
the city nearly all of his animals were dead, and not
only his guns but all the public conveyances of the
army were dragged by the troops.   Ultimately he
was obliged to destroy the whole of his siege-train
and retreat, his camp being poisoned by the bodies
of starved followers and cattle, and his troops
weakened by want of food.   He must not be blamed.
It is not easy to take an army, even without a mass
of followers, for a hundred miles through a country
where there is neither food nor forage.

In the next year, 1792, Cornwallis decided to try
again, having meanwhile captured several strong
forts which would serve him as advanced bases
and magazines.   The whole force from Bengal and
Bombay exceeded thirty thousand men ; and, as
he advanced, Tippoo as usual burned the whole
country on his line of march.   But the previous
year's operations had given Cornwallis secure bases
within little more than fifty miles of Seringapatam ;
and four marches sufficed to bring his force before
the walls.   Even so, if Tippoo had left a garrison
in the capital and used the rest of his force to harass
the British communications from end to end, Cornwallis would have had much ado to keep his army
in sufficient strength before the walls ; but Tippoo

was proud of his disciplined infantry and of his
fortifications, and preferred to meet the British with
their weapons instead of with his own. The result
was that Cornwallis stormed Seringapatam out of
hand within forty-eight hours, and compelled Tippoo
to sign a treaty which deprived him of half of his
territory and resources.

Now came the war of the French Revolution, a
war above all of French intrigues with every people,
nation and language that might bear England a
grudge. During the ten years which followed the
peace of 1783 there had been little peril to the British
in Hindostan owing to the gathering strength of the
Sikhs, who in 1785 had mastered the whole of the
eastern Punjab from the Jhelum to the Sutlej,
where they formed at once a barrier against any
invasion from the passes on the north-west, and a
dam against the rising flood of the Marathas from
the south. The Marathas had by this time thrown
off the authority of the Peshwa, and broken up
into five practically independent states ; and the
most powerful of their chiefs, Scindia of Gwalior,
had reoccupied Delhi and Agra and had actually
called upon the East India Company to pay tribute
for Bengal to him, as the holder of the old Mogul
capital. A contest between British and Marathas for
the mastery of India was therefore certain, sooner
or later ; but meanwhile the various members

of the late confederacy fought indiscriminately against each other. The whole country was overrun with mercenary bands, eager to sell themselves to the highest bidder; and adventurers of all nations were to be found among them, not the least remarkable of such being an Irish sailor, who became for a time a reigning prince with an army of ten thousand men. Luckily for us these adventurers prevailed upon many of the chiefs to train their armies after the European model, which was a fatal error for them; for, choosing to fight the British with their own weapons, they were bound to deliver themselves into their enemies' hands.

Cornwallis left India in 1793, and was succeeded by Sir John Shore. This well-meaning but feeble gentleman allowed both the Marathas and Tippoo to increase their strength at the expense of the Nizam, the ally of the British, and by his weakness encouraged Tippoo to cultivate relations with the French. In 1798 he was succeeded by a very different kind of man, Lord Mornington, better known as Marquess Wellesley, who speedily made up his mind that the anarchy outside the British dominions must cease, and that to this end British authority must become paramount in India. Tippoo Sahib, being the open ally of the French, was the first enemy to be attacked; and the command of the expedition was entrusted to General Harris with Colonel Arthur Wellesley, Mornington's younger brother, for one of his brigadiers. Harris, knowing Tippoo's trick of devastating his country before an invading army, had to think out some method of neutralising it, for his difficulties of transport and supply were frightful. In all he had 120,000 bullocks to draw supplies and stores for his army, and those bullocks must be fed, or the campaign would go for nothing. To protect them he was obliged to advance in a hollow square, two miles broad and seven miles deep, an extremely cumbersome formation; and yet his only resource was to make feints of an advance in one direction so that Tippoo should destroy the country in that quarter, and then swerve away to a district which Tippoo had spared. This device was successful. By much zig-zagging Harris reached Seringapatam in thirty-two days without mishap, and after a month's siege stormed the city for the last time. Tippoo was killed; Tanjore and the Carnatic were annexed to the British dominions; and Mysore was restored to the Hindu dynasty which had formerly ruled it. Arthur Wellesley was meanwhile left in civil and military command of the province, and during the next two years did excellent service in restoring order in southern India. In particular he took note of the superiority, for purpose of transport, of the Mysore bullocks, which can trot six miles an hour.

Mornington's next step was to endeavour to restore the authority of the Peshwa, so as to keep the Maratha chiefs from fighting with their neighbours ; but two of those chiefs, Scindia and Holkar, evaded all British overtures ; and accordingly an army under General Gerard Lake was sent against Scindia's dominions in the north, and another under General Arthur Wellesley against those in the south. Scindia had a vast number of guns cast under European direction, and twenty thousand infantry trained by European officers ; but Wellesley had thought out the means of beating him whether he should adopt European tactics or the old guerilla warfare— always worrying and never fighting—which was traditional with the Marathas. He would make his campaign in the rainy season, and always attack the enemy when on the march and not when in position, for the Maratha chiefs had the gift of choosing very strong positions. This he could ensure by organising his transport, his supply-service and his pontoon-train to perfection. The rivers being in flood he could always cross them with his pontoons, whereas the Marathas would be stopped by them, so that he could catch his enemy wherever he liked. Moreover, since the Marathas lived on the country, whereas he carried his food with him, he could always wait until hunger drove them from any position they might

have occupied, and then follow them up. This plan
seems very simple when you know it, but it needs a
great general to think out the details of a campaign
in this way. Matters did not turn out exactly as
Wellesley had arranged ; but he beat the Marathas
in a first desperate action at Assaye, where only his
own skill and coolness in the presence of tremendous
odds saved the day ; and in a second action at
Argaum, which victory being crowned by the storm
of the almost inaccessible fortress of Gawilghur
crushed the Maratha power in the south. In the
north Lake likewise stormed Aligarh, captured Agra,
won one victory at Delhi, and then by a second
most desperate action at Laswari broke the might
of Scindia in the north. With Holkar however, who
pursued guerilla tactics, Lake was less successful.
Holkar almost annihilated one of his detachments
under Colonel Monson, though this same Monson
shortly afterwards beat him handsomely at Deig.
Lake himself stormed Deig a little later, but failed
with heavy loss in four several assaults upon Bhurtpore, and was obliged to abandon the attempt and
take up the chase of Holkar, whom he hunted almost
to the Indus before he brought him to terms after
three years of hard warfare. Peace left the British
in possession of Delhi and Agra with the contiguous
tracts on both sides of the Jumna, the whole of the
country between the Jumna and the Ganges, and

the province of Cuttack, or in other words with a
continuous length of territory from Bengal north
and westward to the Upper Jumna, and southward
to the Presidency of Madras. Mornington further
instituted the principle that native states under
British influence should keep no regular troops but
those hired from the Anglo-Indian Government,
should refer all disputes with their neighbours to
British arbitration, and should enter into no negotia-
tions with foreign powers.

Hereby Mornington made himself the re-founder,
if the phrase may be used, of our British Empire in
the East; but his wars had been costly, and his
temper was too imperious to commend itself either
to the Directors of the East India Company or to the
Board of Control which represented the Imperial
Government's authority in India. He was therefore recalled, and was succeeded first by Lord
Cornwallis—who died almost immediately—and then
for a time by Sir George Barlow, the senior member
of the Council.

Meanwhile there suddenly burst upon British
India an unsuspected and appalling danger. Owing
to injudicious interference by officers of the King's
service who held high command in the Madras Army,
regulations were introduced which ignored the caste
marks of the Sepoys. Silently but effectually correspondence was established between the Company's

battalions all over the Presidency ; and a general insurrection was concerted for the autumn of 1806. Favourable circumstances caused the garrison at Vellore to rise prematurely ; when eighteen hundred Sepoys made a general attack upon all the Europeans in the fort, murdered several, and were within an ace of complete success. The situation was saved by Colonel Gillespie of the Nineteenth Light Dragoons, who galloped to the spot with his regiment and two guns, forced an entrance into the fort, rallied the Europeans and destroyed the mutineers almost to a man. They had already succeeded in killing and wounding over two hundred British soldiers, so no mercy was shown to them. The service rendered by Gillespie upon this occasion was beyond estimation great ; and it was a matter of extreme good fortune that such a man—ready, energetic and of almost incredible courage—should have been within reach at such a crisis. But for his bravery and promptitude the entire native army of Madras might have mutinied, and the evil might have spread until it threatened the actual existence of the British in India. With her resources strained to the utmost by the struggle with Napoleon England would have found reconquest a difficult matter ; and in short, but for Gillespie, the mutiny of Vellore might have altered the whole course of European as well as Indian history.

Hardly was this peril passed away, when a trouble, almost incredibly strange and formidable, followed upon it. As the Directors had complained of extravagance and expensive wars, Sir George Barlow thought fit, in a true English spirit, to cut down above all things military expenditure ; and this he did mainly by reducing certain allowances to the officers of the Company's army. Now the discipline of the British officers of that army was in a very bad state. For the King's army the King himself was the fountain of honour, and rewards for good service took the form of the Royal approbation publicly signified, of titles of honour, or of the thanks of both Houses of Parliament. The Company's army (except in rare instances) received only the thanks of the Directors—a parcel of merchants in Leadenhall Street—which were naturally little valued ; except so far as they were supplemented by grants of money, of which the officers, condemned to long exile in an unhealthy climate, were very justly tenacious. Hence they had instituted the practice of passing votes of appreciation and approbation of each other, which was most pernicious to discipline. This might rightly have been put down with a strong hand ; but the reduction of pecuniary allowances was a real grievance ; and the officers met it with a number of absurd and insubordinate resolutions. Barlow was a strong and determined man, but he

hated soldiers ; and, instead of appealing to the
better feelings of the officers and using tact as well
as firmness, he sent spies among them, suspended
them arbitrarily right and left without trial, and
employed emissaries to wean the devotion of the
Sepoys from their regimental officers—this last an
inconceivably dangerous measure. To be brief,
in 1809 he succeeded in driving the officers into
open mutiny, which was not suppressed without
bloodshed ; and in fact the trouble was only ended
by the advent of his successor, Lord Minto ; the
officers yielding readily to him but declining altogether to submit to Sir George Barlow. The ill-
feeling bred by this mutiny lasted for thirty years,
and was not without its effect upon the greater
Mutiny of 1857.

To return to more general matters, the policy
of the Directors in holding aloof from affairs outside
their own territory produced the worst consequences.

Lord Minto, equally with Barlow, shrank from
any imitation of Lord Wellesley's masterful keeping
of the peace. The result was that Central India
became the resort of large bands of free-booters,
who ultimately rallied themselves, thirty thousand
strong, under the name of Pindaris, with a single
leader Amir Khan, and bade fair to destroy the
Rajputs, who were our friends, altogether. The
danger was the greater, inasmuch as the beaten

Maratha leaders were chafing under their defeat, and were likely to use the Pindaris as allies. Central India in fact was in a most deplorable condition, when Minto was succeeded in 1814 by Lord Moira, better known as Marquess Hastings, a very able soldier and a resolute man, who realised at once that anarchy must be stopped in Hindostan, otherwise something worse than anarchy might result from it. His first trouble was with the Nepalis or Gurkhas, who were encroaching upon British lands in Bengal and in 1814 actually seized two districts. Hastings at once resolved upon war, and sent an army to penetrate the passes into the mountains. The expedition is noteworthy, for it was the first of our many invasions into the great hill ranges which surround the north of India. The operations were not easy; and it was necessary to invade the frontier in four different columns, varying in strength from four to eight thousand men. One of these was thrice repulsed in attacks upon a hill-fort; and Gillespie, its commander, was killed. There were slight reverses in other parts also, for some of the British officers showed anything but ability; but all was redeemed by the brilliant conduct of General David Ochterlony, commanding the most westerly of the four divisions, who broke through the whole of the Gurkha defences before him, and forced them in the summer of 1815 to sue for peace.

Hostilities were renewed, however, the next year, when Ochterlony, now in supreme command, by further operations drove the Gurkhas to submission. They ceded to us a long tract of the Lower Himalayas, and thus our frontier was brought up to that of the Chinese Empire. Since then there has been unbroken friendship between England and Nepal; and there are no more loyal, efficient and gallant troops in the Imperial service than the Gurkhas.

Meanwhile the situation in Central India had grown worse and worse; and the Pindaris, secretly abetted by the Maratha chiefs, made inroads upon British territory within Bengal and Madras. The Rajputs implored the help of Hastings, who in 1817 set over one hundred thousand men in motion, more than forty thousand from the Dekhan, and more than sixty thousand from Hindostan. The occasion was worthy of so large a force, for three of the Maratha chiefs, Peshwa, Holkar and Bonsla, had thrown in their lot with the Pindaris. The Marathas were speedily weakened by three defeats at Kirki, Sitabaldi and Mahidpur; and part of the armies were then turned upon the Pindaris in converging columns, so as to break them up completely. Defeat after defeat of these free-booters followed, for every man's hand was against them. For years, owing to the timidity of Minto, they had ridden roughshod over the unhappy villagers with murder,

torture and rapine, but now their time was come.
This campaign is the second instance of the employment of the British cavalry in marches of astonishing
length and swiftness to exterminate bands of
brigands. Arthur Wellesley had set the example in
1800, and it was worthily followed now. Very
soon but one formidable band of Pindaris was left
under a leader named Chitu, who was hunted for
days and weeks until he was driven at last into the
jungle and killed by a tiger. The remnant of the
Peshwa's Marathas was again defeated at Korigaon ;
his strongholds fell one after another ; and at length
in March, 1819, the war was brought to an end.
The boundaries of the Maratha states were carefully defined ; their predatory system was utterly
abolished ; and their territories were made subject
to Wellesley's principle with regard to troops,
disputes with neighbours and relations with foreign
powers. Then for the first time for nearly two
centuries there was peace in Central India.

There were now but two points of disturbance
on the British frontier : in the north-west, where the
genius of Ranjit Singh had united the Sikhs into
a single powerful and essentially military nation by
conquest ; and in the north-east, where the Burmese
armies had carried aggression so far as to invade
border-states under British protection. The ill-
deeds of these last caused Lord Amherst, the

Governor-General, to send in 1824 a formidable force of eleven thousand men against them. Few expeditions have been undertaken with more fatuous contempt of information and enquiry than this one. The army was sent by sea to Rangoon with orders to ascend the Irrawadi by water, capturing all the principal cities which lie upon its banks, and so penetrating to Ava. As the province of Pegu, in which Rangoon stands, was a comparatively recent conquest of the Burmese, it was assumed that the inhabitants would be friendly and native supplies plentiful. On the contrary the troops found Rangoon deserted, no boats, no native pilots, no supplies, and were obliged to remain in and about the city, eating such salted and preserved provisions as they had brought with them, until a fresh supply could be brought from India. This accordingly they did, only making occasional sorties to prevent the Burmese from hemming them in altogether. These were costly little operations, for the Burmese threw up stockades with astonishing skill and swiftness, and these required to be stormed. On several occasions attacks upon them were repulsed with loss. Having arrived at the beginning of the rainy season in order to have plenty of water to ascend the river, the British had to endure all the misery and unhealthiness of the rains, aggravated by bad food, with the result that sickness made havoc of the troops and

reduced their effective numbers at one moment to
three thousand men. The Burmese closed in upon
them in force ; but in December, 1824, were driven
back by a general attack upon their whole line.

When the news of the situation reached Calcutta
the Government sent out two additional expeditions
to invade the province of Ava overland, one from
Manipur, the other from Chittagong. The first
route was found impracticable, owing to the density
of the forest ; the second force, eleven thousand
strong, advanced upon Aracan and captured it, but
failed, from neglect of sound geographical information, to find a way to the army on the Irrawadi,
which it had been intended to join, and remained
helpless and stationary.   One fourth of the men died
during the rainy season of 1825, and half of the
survivors were in hospital. The main army meanwhile advanced up the Irrawadi into the interior,
captured Prome, and after several smart actions
arrived within sixty miles of Ava, when the Burmese
at the beginning of 1826 met them and made
submission. Assam, Aracan and Tennasserim were
ceded to the British, and thus some compensation
was gained for a very costly and destructive
campaign. The casual fashion in which war had
been begun in a region of continuous marsh and
forest at the beginning of the rainy season, when
the whole country was inundated, was thoroughly

English and most condemnable. Thousands of lives were sacrificed which might have been saved, and it was fortunate that matters fell out no worse than they did. Meanwhile the eternal assault of stockades was very trying to the troops, and gave opportunities, which were abundantly taken, for brilliant displays of valour.

While this was going on, the throne of Bhurtpore became vacant through the death of the Rajah, and was usurped by a pretender. This was a direct menace to the peace of India; and Sir David Ochterlony, who was the Resident at Delhi, at once assembled a force to drive out the usurper. So little, however, did the Governor-General know his duty, that he countermanded the project and publicly censured Ochterlony in terms of extravagant harshness. The veteran General resigned, but was so much affected by Amherst's foolish policy and by the slight put upon himself that he died soon afterwards. Then of course Amherst was obliged to do at last what he should have done at first, and Sir Stapleton Cotton was sent with twenty thousand men to besiege the famous fortress which had foiled the eager impetuosity of Lake. Its strength may be imagined by the statistics that its circuit is five miles in extent, that the ditch of the citadel was fifty yards wide and fifty feet deep, and that the ramparts generally, besides being of great height and thickness, were built of clay which refused to crumble away under the battering of round shot. A bastion was therefore undermined and blown up, and the place was stormed out of hand.

Lord Amherst was succeeded in 1828 by Lord William Bentinck, a man who, having had Macaulay to write his epitaph, enjoys a reputation far above his deserts. He was mediocre alike as soldier and statesman, and had an extraordinary knack of doing foolish things. While Governor-General his only idea was to save money for the Directors—he even tried to sell the Taj Mahal, the gem of Mohammedan architecture in India ;—but he neglected to keep the peace ; he reduced the allowances of the European officers, in direct breach of agreement ; and finally, to curry favour with the humanitarians, he, in the face of all advice from British and native soldiers, abolished the punishment of the lash in the native regiments. The mischief which he thus did was incalculable ; for he lowered the officers in the eyes of the natives, and so ruined the discipline of the Sepoys that beyond doubt he was the greatest of all contributors to the Mutiny of 1857. The Duke of Wellington, and all who knew India, were furious with him ; but being a sentimental Whig, which is synonymous with a man of good intentions and bad judgement, he found and still finds many admirers at home. Let me beg you not to be carried away by their admiration. Bentinck certainly did some good work, but an Indian administrator who ruins the discipline of the army—and Bentinck undoubtedly did so—is not only no statesman, but a foolish and mischievous person.

Bentinck was succeeded by Lord Auckland, whose name, unfortunately for him, is bound up with the greatest of our military disasters in India. Since the fall of Napoleon Russia had steadily pursued her advance eastwards, and by 1828 had not only appropriated some of the western territory of Persia but had gained paramount influence in that country. Thus we found ourselves confronted with the probability that we should presently have an European Power of colossal strength for our neighbour ; and the question was how she should be kept at arm's length. The Government resolved that a barrier must be formed in Afghanistan. That country had lately passed out of the line of the creator of the Afghan kingdom into the hands of a strong and competent usurper. Since Persia threatened to indemnify herself for the territory lost to Russia by encroachment upon Afghanistan, this usurper, Dost Mohammed, was anxious for the English alliance. Lord Auckland on the contrary preferred to support the legitimate sovereign, Shah Shuja, who was an exile in the Punjab, and decided to replace him on the throne by an armed force, on

the assumption that such an ally would be surer than
Dost Mohammed.   The operation was one of extreme
danger, for the British and Afghan boundaries were
hundreds of miles apart. Our base of operations was
Scinde, a foreign state under rulers unfriendly to
us ; and full upon our flank, able at any moment
to cut us off from India, lay the Sikhs, equally a
foreign state, nominally amicable but really very
jealous, and in possession of a powerful army.

A treaty was made with the Amirs of Scinde
whereby we obtained the right to use the navigation
of the Indus.   With enormous difficulty transport
and supplies were brought up to feed the armies
during the march through the barren passes of
Afghanistan ; and, after frightful losses of animals
and no small peril of starvation, some fifteen thousand men and twenty thousand followers marched
by the Bolan and Khojak passes to Kandahar,
opened the way from thence to the capital by the
storm of Ghazni ; and in August, 1839, escorted
Shah Shuja into Kabul.   Then the difficulties began.
It was very soon evident that, without a British
force, Shah Shuja's reign would be short ; so one
division of infantry and a little cavalry and artillery
were left to occupy the country, and the rest of the
army marched for India. Honours were lavished
on the commanders, and everyone flattered himself
that the work was done. Signs of insurrection,

however, soon showed themselves; and the British troops scattered about between Kabul, Ghazni, Kandahar and Jelalabad were incessantly employed in putting down tribal risings. By the autumn of 1840 the commander of the army of occupation was crying out for reinforcements. The winter of 1840–1 passed away fairly quietly, and not until the following November did the final insurrection at Kabul occur. The general in command there was weak and incompetent; and the whole of his division was cut to pieces. Ghazni and various small forts were captured; and, though Jelalabad and Kandahar were stoutly held, all communication with India was hopelessly cut off. It was necessary to send practically a fresh army to relieve the beleaguered garrisons; but the Indian Government was at first so panic-stricken as to lose all thought of anything but the immediate withdrawal of the army of occupation. The Governor-General, Lord Ellenborough, who had succeeded Auckland, later bethought him that such a timid retreat would endanger our whole Empire in India, but had not courage to order a new advance upon Kabul. Happily the generals took the responsibility which their superiors feared to incur. They did not withdraw their armies until they had forced their way triumphantly, the one by the Khyber Pass and Jelalabad, the other from Kandahar, to Kabul. Then and not till then did they evacuate

Afghanistan, having shown that the British were still unconquerable. Even so the principle upon which the operations were conducted was open to much criticism, though everything was redeemed by the gallant behaviour of the troops.

While withdrawing from Afghanistan, however, Lord Ellenborough was anxious to retain our hold upon the lower Indus with the fort of Karachi, which had been occupied temporarily as our base for the late operations. Sir Charles Napier was therefore sent out to Scinde with a small force to press upon the Amirs a treaty to that effect. The Amirs very naturally resented the demand; whereupon Napier instantly struck the first blow. His campaign is one which every Englishman should know, and which none has any excuse for not knowing; for its history was written by William Napier. Charles Napier began by making a raid with five hundred and fifty men mounted on camels across many miles of desert to a stronghold of the Amirs, and blowing up the fort with gunpowder. On this march he carried not only provisions but water for the whole force, animals and men. Then returning to the Indus he marched south upon Hyderabad with twenty-eight hundred men; and on the 17th of March, 1843, attacked between twenty and thirty thousand of the enemy at Miani, in a strong position above the bed of a dry river. There followed one of the greatest and most marvellous battles ever fought by the British ; and at the close of three hours the enemy was hopelessly routed with a loss of five thousand men. Again the Baluchis managed to collect twenty thousand men ; and Napier, having been reinforced to a strength of five thousand men, defeated them in a second action of much the same kind at Dubba ; after which he with little more trouble completed the subjection of the Amirs. Scinde was then annexed ; and Napier as its first Governor showed himself not less capable as an administrator than as a general.

By this time trouble had arisen in the dominions of Scindia owing to the death of the Maharaja without issue ; and an armed insurrection broke out against the authority of the Regent accepted by the British Government. The matter was one which at ordinary times might have been adjusted by patience ; but the attitude of the Sikhs, which I shall describe immediately, was such that there could be no trifling. The Maratha armies had been assembled, some thirty thousand strong, including between them twenty-two thousand men trained by European officers ; and, with a disputed succession in train, it was impossible to say what mischief their leaders might work. Ellenborough therefore ordered a strong force to enter Scindia's dominions in two columns, and the war was ended

in one day—29th of Dec. 1843—by the simultaneous
victories of Sir Hugh Gough at Maharajpore, and
of General Grey at Punniar. These were the last of
our battles with the Marathas. They have never
to this day forgiven us for depriving them of the
mastery of India; and in 1843, in consequence of
our defeats in Afghanistan, they had been stirring
up hostility against us in every court of the East.
The double defeat therefore gave them a salutary
lesson.

Lord Ellenborough was now recalled; and
Sir Henry Hardinge, one of Wellington's veterans
and a highly accomplished soldier, came out as
Governor-General in his stead. The condition of
the Punjab was most critical. Ranjit Singh, the
great leader and ruler of the Sikhs, had died in 1839,
leaving no strong man to succeed him. The succession was of course disputed; and a course of
risings, mutinies and assassinations showed that the
great Sikh state was sinking into anarchy. All
power had passed into the hands of committees of
regimental officers, who were in turn partly controlled
by the passions of their men. The nominal ruler
could think of no better resource than to turn the
unruly host across the Sutlej to fight the English,
for which some recent frontier disputes furnished
sufficient pretext. Lord Hardinge, who had seen
what was coming, was ready for them, and some

twelve thousand men under Sir Hugh Gough advanced to meet them. Sir Hugh was a very brave man but a very bad commander, who could not see a wall without dashing his head against it. In the first action, Moodkee, he hurried his troops into the fight with every disadvantage, and though victorious lost nine hundred men. In the second action three days later at Ferozeshah, he launched about sixteen thousand British and Sepoys against fifty thousand Sikhs in a very strong position, and was practically beaten at the close of the first day's fighting, though he recovered himself on the second. In this affair he threw away twenty-five hundred men ; and on the night after the first engagement the British Empire in India rocked for some hours on the verge of ruin. A month later a far more telling and scientific victory was won by Sir Harry Smith with a detachment of the army at Aliwal ; and then Gough made a final blundering attack upon the Sikhs in a strongly entrenched position at Sobraon, where, though the valour of his troops and the devotion of his divisional generals won a decisive victory, it was at a cost once more of nearly twenty-five hundred men.

Sobraon brought the war for the moment to a close ; but the government temporarily established by us in the Punjab was weak and inefficient ; and early in 1848 a general insurrection brought about

a reassembling of the Sikh army to try conclusions
with the British once more. Lord Dalhousie, the
new Governor-General, at once took up the challenge;
and Gough again was in command of the army. He
began as usual by knocking his head against a very
strong position of the Sikhs at Ramnuggar, and was
repulsed. He did precisely the same thing a few
weeks later at Chillianwalla, once more lost nearly
twenty-five hundred men, and fought at best a
drawn battle. Finally a month later he fought a
third action at Gujerat on the 21st of February, 1849,
showed for once (he or his officers for him) some
tactical skill, and won a great and decisive victory
with comparatively small loss. The Punjab was
then annexed to the British dominions by Dalhousie,
and the frontier thus carried to the foot of the mountains of Afghanistan. But the struggle had been
very severe, for the Sikhs were most valiant men,
very skilful gunners, and masters of the art of
choosing strong positions, whereas Gough was a hot-
headed Irishman, of splendid bravery, but wholly
unfit to command anything larger than a battalion
in action.

But still there was no rest for the British Army.
Doubtless under the spell of our disasters in Afghanistan, the Burmese Government had been bullying
and maltreating British merchants at Rangoon in
violation of the treaty of 1826 ; and its only response

to Dalhousie's protests was contemptuous insult
to his envoys. An expedition was therefore despatched to Rangoon in 1852, which first and last
numbered some twenty thousand men ; but on
this occasion the campaign was properly thought
out. A few towns only, which commanded the
mouth of the Irrawadi, were captured so as to cut
off all external trade, and within eighteen months
the Court of Ava was obliged to sue for peace.
The fighting was of slight importance, indeed the
sharpest was against dacoits or patriot banditti,
some of whom were very formidable. However,
the Government at Calcutta took care to provide
land-transport, in case an inland advance should be
necessary, elephants in particular being employed
in very large numbers. The province of Pegu
was annexed to the British dominions, and thereupon followed a brief period of peace, during which
Dalhousie annexed also three Maratha states, in
default of direct heirs, and the Kingdom of Oudh.

It was this period of peace, signifying practically
the pacification of all India, that brought about
the mutiny of the Sepoys of the Bengal Army.
There were various contributory causes, most notably
the steady decay of its discipline, partly through
the employment of the best officers in political
work, and the making of political services the best
channel to advancement, partly owing to the steady

discouragement of the officers in favour of the men which had marked the mistaken policy of Bentinck. The Sepoys were so continually flattered that they imagined themselves to have conquered India, whereas without European battalions an Indian army is like a spear without a point. They therefore broke out into mutiny, and for a time extinguished British rule in certain districts. Thereupon reappeared all the old animosities of past centuries, Mohammedan and Hindu fighting each other more fiercely than the English; while adventurers joyfully gathered bands of their own kind around them for the gay business of free-booting. Great part of the country settled down to a hearty enjoyment of anarchy; and nearly two years were needed to restore order. Two regiments indeed, the Central India Horse, were raised on purpose to hunt down banditti in Central India, and are still always the first troops to be sent into the field wherever there is serious police-duty to be done.

In 1858 the East India Company was swept out of existence, and the Crown took over all its forces and the entire business of administration in India. With a frontier conterminous with the highlands from which warlike tribes have from time immemorial descended to raid the plains, we have since been obliged to make endless expeditions to punish the raiders, all very difficult operations and some of

them very costly. Umbeyla, Bhotan, Beluchistan,
Tirah, Chitral, Tibet are names which recall some of
these campaigns; and in 1878 the exclusion of a
British mission from Afghanistan while a Russian
mission was received at Kabul brought on a second
and serious Afghan War. As in 1838, Kabul was
reached with little difficulty; and the battle only
began, after peace had been made, with an insurrection in the capital. There was no such disaster as
in 1841, for we captured Kabul and Kandahar at
once; yet we were absolutely powerless to subdue
and pacify the whole country. We suffered one
serious reverse; and our difficulties would have
been endless had there not been at hand a strong
man whom we installed as ruler of the country,
and under whose iron hand the most refractory
tribesmen trembled and were still. Lastly in 1885
the Burmese having again insulted us, an expedition
was sent which made its way without difficulty to
Mandalay. Upper Burma was annexed to the
British dominions, and there followed two weary
years spent in suppressing marauding bands and
free-booters. The operations of these two years
have been called the subalterns' war, for they were
conducted mainly by very small parties under the
leadership of subalterns, who made their way with
indomitable perseverance through the jungle by
native paths, and, being generally at the head of

the column, were lamentably often picked off by
the shot of an unseen enemy.

Altogether the exploits of the British in the
conquest of India form a very remarkable story,
though it is by no means unchequered by follies,
failures and misconduct. We very early learned
that we must never retreat before Orientals, but
must always attack, no matter what the odds against
us ; and by following this rule we have under able
commanders achieved most astonishing feats of
war. In particular is the record of the British regiments remarkable. The East Indian European Army
was enlisted for short service, though it contained
many old soldiers in its ranks ; but the British
soldier of the King's regiments was enlisted for at
least twenty-one years, if not for life, and his prowess
is amazing. You know of course that it is rare for
a battalion of any army to be fit for much, after
suffering severe loss in action, until its ranks
have been refilled. But the British battalions, led
by Lake, Wellesley and Gough, though they rarely
took the field more than six hundred strong, would
lose one hundred and fifty men in a fight on Monday,
two hundred more in another fight on Thursday,
and over one hundred more in a third fight on
Thursday fortnight. Nothing seemed to have power
to stop them, at any rate in India. Time after time
in the assault of hill-fortresses in the south the

Sepoys failed, and a few companies of British were brought forward to show them how to do the work. No losses seemed to daunt them. Individual men served in storming party after storming party, and would not wait to be healed of wounds received in a first assault before they volunteered to risk almost certain death in a second.

Still, as I have said, there are records of many failures and we are too fond of passing over our weak points and dwelling on the strong. In the case of the Mutiny we recall with pride the deeds of Nicholson and Havelock, and are never weary of the old stories of the siege of Delhi and the relief of Lucknow. All honour to those who quitted themselves like men ; but I am afraid there are many episodes of the Mutiny which are little credit-able to the British, whether civilians or soldiers. A great many individuals were found unequal to the occasion ; and this is true of every war and probably of the majority of actions. There was certainly one instance of misbehaviour at Trafalgar, one ship did not respond to Nelson's famous signal ; and Collingwood spoke his mind about it at the time, though few people know it. We must therefore never be satisfied with the fame of our fore-runners, and suppose that it suffices for us. Let us by all means be kindled by their example to the utmost fulfilment of our duty ; but let us know also when

and where and why they failed. Let us study
their defeats as well as their victories ; let us ask
ourselves whether some of the failings which brought
about those defeats may not still be present among
us. If we can truly and conscientiously say that
they are not, then we may—but always with
caution—presume to criticise and even to censure ;
always remembering that it is not enough for us
to emulate the deeds of our ancestors. If we are
not to fall below them, we must endeavour to
surpass them, for there is no such thing as a
stationary Empire.

INDEX

www.ingramcontent.com/pod-product-compliance
Ingram Content Group UK Ltd.
Pitfield, Milton Keynes, MK11 3LW, UK
UKHW042143280225
455719UK00001B/61